CW00919536

PREFACE

The third addition of the book is in your hands. This book is written within the blend of the religion of Islam and child psychology without losing the taste of either. I have not manipulated, modified, or extrapolated any fact from the religion of Islam with the child psychology just to prove my point. Whatever I have said in the book is nothing but part of the Qur'an and the Sunnah of Mohammed (s). To make the book more resourceful, I have provided ample references from the most reliable and authentic resources such as the Qur'an and the Ahadith for my readers. For example, I have started every chapter of the book with my own comments and concluded it with relevant reference(s). So if readers have any doubt as to my opinion, they can verify it from the given resource.

A self-assessment test for parents is another interesting aspect I have incorporated in this book for my readers. Answer these questions before and after you read the book. Compare your score before and after reading and assess if you have learned anything. You will not need answers to these questions after reading the complete book. I, however, have provided answers somewhere in the book for the reader's convenience.

If you scored below the satisfactory level before reading the book, do not dismay. The book must broaden the spectra of your visibility in true parenting. You should score well after reading the book. Honestly speaking, I could not rate myself within the level of "exceptional parents" when I took the test after writing it. We are human beings. Thus, we have a certain level of understanding as well as some limitations. We, however, should be open minded and willing to work to become good parents.

I am open to suggestions, complaints, comments, and compliments from readers. As I have spent many years putting this informative and resourceful book together for you, please take a few minutes of your time and write me back with your feelings about the book.

In the end, I pray to Allah (S), "O-Allah (S)! accept my effort to provide good parenting guidelines or guide me otherwise."

Sincerely,

JAVED KHAN,
615 E. Monterey Road
Corona, CA 92879
951-616-4241
tabishkhanzada@msn.com

ABOUT THE BOOK

Below is the feedback from the previous two editions of this book:

"You have done a marvelous job in collecting and presenting a parenting guideline from the Qur'an for Muslim parents." **Dr. Justice Javed Iqbal S/O Allama Mohammed Iqbal, Lahore, Pakistan.**

"We should thank the author for using this fascinating approach to such an important subject." **Dr. Ahmad Sakar.**

"The text is well-interpreted with relevant quotes from the Qur'an and Ahadith. This book is full of wisdom and guidance. I would recommend this book for everybody planning to get married." **ILM- Islamic Research Foundation.**

"In this book, the author covers the important topic of raising children in an Islamic way and with the guidance provided by the Qur'an and Ahadith. The book is useful reading for parents and can also be very informative for youngsters." **The Orange Crescent (Aug. 1994)**

"This is the book that should be in every Muslim house and should be read by every Muslim parent." **Raza Iqbal, IC, Berkeley.**

"I have found this book most helpful for the education of both parents and children." **Jamshed Hussain, IC, Delaware.**

"This book has answered a lot of my questions. I thank the author very much for writing this book." **Sis. Nasira Chaudhary, IC, San Francisco.**

"In general, this book holds a new approach in rearing children. This book is written for both parents and children." **Sis. Nazik Younis, IC, Ohio.**

"This is a worthwhile reading book: both for parents and children. Like traditional Islamic books, this book does not bore its readers.." **Agha Babur**

(late), NY.

"This book satisfies it readers from Islamic and parenting point of view." **Ijaz Hussain Batalvie, Advocate Pakistan Supreme Courts.**

"Author deserves our thanks for writing such a book for Muslim parents." **Mehboob Ilahi, Founding member of Pakistan Muslim League, New Jersey.**

"The author deserves the highest commendation for guiding parents in rearing children in the sublime of the Qur'an and Hadith."
Dr. Sajjad **Haider, Human Development consultant, N.B. Indiana.**

ACKNOWLEDGEMENTS

I thank all who read the first editions and sent me suggestions, concerns, and compliments. Many of my readers and Islamic scholars sent me feedback on the first editions. This edition reflects suggested changes. I am specially thankful to:

Justice Dr. Javed Iqbal, Agha Babur, A. Rehman Siddique, Faiz Rehman, Dr. Ahmad Sakker, Dr. Sajjad Haider, and Advocate Ijaz Husain Batalvie for feedback.

Teresa Anderson, Cosette Larsen, Samantha Vaughn, and Fatima Khan for proofreading.

This book is dedicated to Parents like us.

A SELF-ASSESSMENT TEST FOR PARENTS

1   Do you spend enough quality time with your family?
2   Do you prefer your family over your friends?
3   Do you love your son more than your daughter?
4   Do you show love and respect for your children in overt and covert ways?
5   Do you show love and respect for your parents in overt and covert ways?
6   Do you exhibit love and respect for your children in front of your parents?
7   Do you exhibit love and respect for your parents in front of your children?
8   Do you allow your parents to live with you?
9   Do you allow your parents to live with you only to baby-sit your children?
10   Do you love some of your children more than the others?
11   Do you treat all of your children equally?
12   Do you sometimes act disrespectfully towards your parents in front of your children?
13   Do you play with your children?
14   Do you let your children make their own decisions in all aspect of their lives?
15   Do you have positive relationships with your children?
16   Do you tend to make your children scared of you?
17   Do you hit or spank your children for no good reason?
18   Do you educate your children about sex?
19   Do you feel satisfied with the upbringing of your children?
20   Do you have any criteria to choose a baby-sitter?
21   Do you ever force your children to lie for you?

"Parenting in Islam" By Javed I Khan

22   Do you feel embarrassed to introduce your parents to your friends?

23   Do you practice what you preach with your children?

24   Do you show love and respect for other people's parents?

25   Do you show love and respect for other people's children?

26   Do you teach your children to respect elders?

27   Do you show your love to your children frequently?

28   Do you show your love to your parents frequently?

29   Do you show love for your children openly?

30   Do you support your family with your prayer?

31   Do you guide your children towards the straight path?

32   Do you pray for the success of your children?

33   Do you pray for the forgiveness of your parents?

34   Do you thank Allah (S) for giving you such a nice family and loving children?

35   Do you follow your motherly instincts about your children?

36   Do you want to see your children as cowards?

37   Do you yell at your children when they betray your trust?

38   Do you support your impasse adult children?

39   Do you give a second chance to children?

40   Do you pay undivided attention to the children when they talk with you?

41   Do you brag about the children in front of your friends and family?

42   Do you hide your children's weak points from your spouse?

43   Does your spouse favor the children when you are mad at them?

44   Would you commit any minor or major crime for the sake your children?

45   Would you commit any minor or major crime for the sake

your parents?

46   Would you commit any sin for the sake of your parents?

47   Would you commit any sin for the sake of your children?

48   Would you like to be imprisoned for your child's crime?

49   Would you like to be imprisoned for your parent's crime?

50   Would you prefer to have a son rather than a daughter?

GLOSSARY OF ABBREVIATIONS

I have used the following abbreviations (abb.) after the name of Allah (S), the Prophets (As) and other elite Islamic figures. Meaning of the abbreviations are given below:

ABB.   READ   MEANING

(S)   سبحانهٗ وتعالیٰ   The Sacred and The Mighty

(s)   (صل اللہ تعالیٰ ہو علیہ وصلم)   Peace be upon him

(A)   علیہ سلام   May Allah (S) bless him

(R)   رضی اللہ تعالیٰ   May Allah (S) be pleased with him

(r)   رحمت اللہ علیہ   May Allah's (S) mercy be upon him

Ahadith   Mohammed's (s) Saying

Sunnah   Practical aspects of Mohammed's (s) life

X(Y) (Chapter)   X = Number of Sura Quran

                            Y = Number of Ayah (Verse)

TABLE OF CONTENTS

"Parenting in Islam" By Javed I Khan

PART III: RIGHTS OF PARENTS

13

PART IV: CHILDREN OF EARLY ISLAM

15

INTRODUCTION

My research, thoughts, and understanding towards parenting could be concluded in a few sentences: Ambiance and God-given are the only two factors involved in child rearing. Ambiance is the contribution of society, parents, school, friends and other related environment. The effects of this factor on child rearing, however, are very limited but very crucial. God seems to be the major and dominant factor in the entire game of raising children. Both factors, no doubt, play very vital roles collectively.

If (s)he is not insane, every parent on the face of the earth carries the desire to be the most loving and caring parent there has ever been. Each of the parents wishes to know their children as obedient, intelligent, well-cared, well-behaved, well-organized, well-disciplined, gifted and the most loved children in the world. If raising desirable children were solely in the parents' hands, they would have raised marvelous children. As a result, the whole world would have been a perfect, crime free, and peaceful place to live. Regardless of parenting or non-parenting, disciplining or non-disciplining, caring or carelessness, loving or hating, children seem to have equal chances of becoming good or bad. I would like to prove my points from the history of the world and from the history of Islam in the following two paragraphs:

Looking into the role of the parents of most influential individuals like Quaid-E-Azam, Albert Einstein, George Washington, and Abraham Lincoln- I concluded that the parents' role is crucial but not effective enough to bring up the child(ren) at the altitude of changing the course of the history of mankind.

Moreover, a small minority knows about the parents of these elites. Above all, none of these elite was an only child. Some had other siblings and most people of the present time have very little or no knowledge about their sibling.

The history of Islam also shows the same picture of parenting. The Qur'an has narrated the story of the Prophet Abraham (A), whose father was not only an idol-worshiper, but was also an idol-maker and was against his own son's ideology of Islam. The Qur'an also states that Prophet Noah's (A) son was among the losers. Nobody among the readers will dare to credit Aazar, Abraham's (A) father, and degrade Noah (A) on the basis of child rearing.

Mohammed (s) was born a few months after his father's death and his mother died when he was just a seven-years-old boy. He (s) was raised amongst the idol worshippers. Who guided him and made him the leader of the world? Certainly, there is some power behind the scene and that power seems to be the real source of guidance and success. Allah (S) is that power and the rest (parents, teachers, friends, society, etc.) are His tools and resources that He may or may not use sometimes.

To help parents, child psychologists have developed some important guidelines for parenting mentally, emotionally, spiritually, and physically healthy children. By following these guidelines, the chances of bringing up quality children could be maximized. The identical guidelines had already been revealed in the Qur'an more than fourteen-hundred-years ago. I have many good reasons to believe that the Qur'an is the ultimate, comprehensive, precise, and a distinguished resource of guidance for each and every aspect of human life- including parenting. By

18

following these guidelines, we can successfully raise physically, mentally, emotionally, and spiritually healthy children. Moreover, these children can bring us the success and happiness in this life and in the life hereafter.

In this book, I have gathered the scattered parenting guidelines from the Qur'an, from the life of Mohammed (s), and from the history of Islam. I, then, related this information to the existing psychological rules of raising children of the modern age. I have divided this book into four parts: The first part of the book is about family structure, spousal selection and the beginning of parenting from the Islamic point of view.

The second part of the book reflects on the rights of children over parents in Islam and is the focal point of this book. In this part of the book, we shall see Mohammed (s) who was a loving father and grandfather- beside he was the Prophet of Allah (S). In addition, he was a distinguished army general, a truthful, and an honest businessman. We shall, also see the fatherly faces of other Prophets like Abraham, Zakariya, Noah, and Lot (As). We shall glance into the childhood of these and other Prophets (As) through the mirror of the Qur'an and Hadith as well. This part of the book can be summarized that taking good care and showing affection towards all children is one of the most commendable deeds in Islam. According to a Hadith, *"It is a charity of a high order to attend to their educational needs and teach them proper manners (Al-Muslim)."* Interest in the responsibility for child welfare is a high priority in Islam. According to Mohammed's (s) instructions, *"Children should be given a pleasant and good name by the seventh day of birth, and their heads should be shaved, along with all other hygienic measures required for good health. Also, silver or gold, equal to the weight of the shaved hair, should be given to the poor in charity."*

Parents are jointly responsible for the upbringing of the children. The father is a provider and the mother is a nurturer in a good Muslim family. The children must be provided with adequate and healthy care under the supervision of both parents and a nanny (if affordable). The parents together shall attend to the mental, emotional, and spiritual growth and socialization of their children. Mohammed (s) urged parents to require their children to practice Islam beginning early in life. For example, children should start praying by the age of seven and should start praying regularly (five times a day) by the age of ten.

The third part of the book gives us the knowledge of duties of children towards parents. We shall learn -as adults- as how to treat our parents rightly. The last part of the book has been selected from Islamic history. In this part of the book, we shall learn the role of the young companions of Mohammed (s). The purpose of this part of the book is to remind our youngsters that they can make a big difference in this world as our early young Muslims did. Young Muslims have played very important and distinguished roles in the history of Islam. On many occasions, children saved life of Mohammed (s). More than ninety percent of the Ahadith and the Sunnah were transmitted to us through Mohammed's (s) young companions. Thus, if it were not for this young, active, and energetic group of the companions of Mohammad (s), we might not have this religion in its present form. The time that this group of companions spent with the Prophet (s) varied. Some of them spent their entire youth, some a few years, some a few days, and yet some only a few moments in the company of the Prophet (s). Their age varied from two to the early twenties at the time of the Prophet's (s) death. To inspire our young generation, to repeat history once again, and to make a difference in the modern world, I have provided the best collection of true stories of these youngsters and their important roles in early Islam.

PART I

RIGHTS OF FAMILY

STAGES OF LIFE

Allah (S) has divided human life into four stages. I am not going to discuss the first stage of life in this book because it deals with a child in mother's womb. The remaining three stages are described separately by Allah (S) in the Qur'an on different occasions:

"O mankind! If you are in doubt concerning the Resurrection, then (remember)! (1) We have created you from dust, then from a drop of sperm, then from a leech-like clot, then from a little lump of flesh partly shaped and partly shapeless, that We may manifest (our power) for you. And We cause what We will to remain in the wombs for an appointed time, (2) and afterward We bring you forth as an infants, (3) then (give you growth) that you attain your full strength. And among you there is he who dies (young), (4) and among you there is he who brought back to the most abject time of his life, so that, after knowledge, he knows not. And you (Mohammed) see the earth barren, but when We send down water thereon, it thrills and swells and put forth every lovely kind (of growth)." 22(5)

"It is He, Who has created you from dust, then from a sperm-drop, then from a leech-like clot; then does He get you out (into the light) as a child: then lets you (grow and) reach your age of full strength; then lets you become old. Though of you there are some who die before; and lets you reach a term appointed; in order that you may understand." 40(67)

"Verily We created man from a drop of mingled sperm, in order to try him. So We gave him (the gifts), of hearing and sight." 76(2)

"Then We made the sperm into a clot of congealed blood; then of that clot We made a lump (fetus); then We made out of that lump bones and clothed the bones with flesh; then We developed out of it another creature. So blessed be Allah, the Best to create. Man we did create from a quintessence (of clay). Then We placed him as (a drop of) sperm in a place of rest, firmly fixed: After that, at length You will die. Again, on the Day of Judgment, will you be raised up." 23(11-16)

"Allah is He Who shaped you out of weakness (child), then made you strong after weakness, then, after strength (youth), appointed weakness and gray hair (old age). He creates what He wills. He is, the Knower, the Mighty." 30(54)

SPOUSAL SELECTION

The selection of a spouse is the most critical step towards good parenting, so should be taken very seriously. The selection of a spouse could be based on wealth, beauty, and/or religion. Mohammed (s) has recommended his followers to consider the beauty of a woman and wealth of a man secondary to religion when selecting a spouse.

Marriage not only brings two individuals together, it also blends two distinct families. There are two common types of marriages: arranged marriages and love-match marriages. Arranged marriage is the most common type of marriage in the Muslim world and is one of the traditions of Mohammed (s). In arranged marriages, not only do two people get to understand each other, also two families get to see the compatibility among themselves. In arranged marriages, however, -individuals to be married- must mutually agree upon to be wed-locked. Any external influence either from parents or anybody else should not be applied in this decision. Parents or family members may act as counselors or advisers, however. If either the girl or the boy does not agree, the marriage is illegal under the Islamic Laws. The enforced marriage IS AN ELICIT ISLAMIC CONDUCT AND SHOULD NOT BE PRACTICED. For example, once a young girl came to Mohammed (s) and pleaded, "My parents enforced my marriage with a person I hate." Mohammed (s) sent for her father and revoked the marriage. *Mohammed (s) also told his companions, "See before you propose to somebody." (Al-Bokhari)*

Love-match marriage is another popular way of marriage among our young and immature generations of this age. These relationships often start up with the blind emotions of passion or lust and end up with the tragedy of divorce. Looking at the divorce rates in the two kind of marriages, arranged marriages seem to be more successful than love-match marriages. There are, however, some exceptions in either type of marriages. Let us see what the Qur'an has said in this regard.

"And (have We not) created you in pairs." 17(85)

"And of everything We have created pairs: That you may reflect." 51(49)

"(He is) the Creator of the heavens and the earth: He has made you in pairs among yourselves, and pairs among cattle: By this means does He multiply you: there is nothing whatever like unto Him, and He is the One that hears and sees." 42(11)

"That He did create the pairs, male and female." 53(45)

'And those who pray, "Our Lord! Grant unto us wives and offspring who will be the comfort of our eyes, and give us (the grace) to lead the righteous."' 25(74)

According to the Qur'an, Allah (S) has created us in pairs, which implies that our to-be-spouse is predetermined. So it is inevitable that everybody shall get a spouse regardless of self-search or family-search method. In my opinion, one should be patient and wait for Allah's (S) decision. His is the best of all decisions. Here, I can relate my personal experience. My patience and prayers to Allah (S) rewarded me with the most wonderful, undergird, and coveted wife that I could ever dream of finding by myself.

Generally speaking, a good person gets a good spouse and a bad person receives a bad spouse. However, there are exceptions to this rule to prove that our mates have already been created by Allah

(S), however. For example, the Qur'an tells us that wives of the Prophet Noah and Lot (As) were disbelievers, while the pharaoh's wife, on the other hand, was a good Muslim. all of the above individuals would have picked a supportive wife for themselves if picking a compatible spouse were in the hands of a person. Below are the references from the Qur'an on this issue.

'Allah sets forth, for an example to the unbelievers, the wife of Noah and the wife of Lot: They were (respectively) under two of your righteous servants but they betrayed their (husbands), And they profited nothing before Allah on their account, but were told: "Enter you the Fire along with (others)!"
And Allah sets forth, as an example to those who believe the wife of Pharaoh. Behold she said: "O my Lord! build for me, in nearness to You, a mansion in the garden, and save me from Pharaoh and his doings, and save me from those that do wrong."' 66(10-11)

"But We saved him {Lot (A)} and his family, except his wife: She was of those who lagged behind." 7(83)

"Except his {Lot (A)} wife, who, We have ascertained, will be among those who will lag behind." 15(60)

"He {Abraham (A)} said: "But there is Lot there." They said: "We know well who is there: we will certainly save him and his followers, except his wife: she is of those who lagged behind." 29(32)

"Behold, We delivered him {Lot (A)} and his adherents, all except an old woman (Lot's Wife) who was among those who lagged behind: Then We destroyed the rest." 37(134-136)

"(He is) The Creator of the heavens and the earth: He has made you in pairs among yourselves, and pairs among cattle: And that's how He multiplies you: there is nothing whatever like Him, and He is the One that hears and sees." 42(11)

SPOUSAL RELATIONSHIP

Once Mohammed (s) told his companions, "I am the best husband among all men." His wife, Aisha, answered to a person inquiring about the conduct of Mohammed (s)," Mohammed (s) had the conduct of the Qur'an," and the Qur'an states, "Mohammed has the most beautiful conduct of all."

On various occasions, the Qur'an has mentioned the spousal relationship in a very respectful, unique, and the most appropriate manner. Below are references from the Qur'an which indicate the beauty of this relationship:

"Your women are tilth for you so go to your tilth as you will, and send (good deeds) before you for your souls and fear Allah and know that you will (one day) meet Him. Give glad tidings to believers, (O Mohammed)." 2(223)

"Beautified for mankind is love of things they covet (that comes) from women (wives) and offspring, and stored-up heaps of gold and silver, and horses branded (with their mark), and cattle and land. That is comfort of the life of the world. Allah! With Him is a more excellent goals." 3(14)

"And among His signs are this, that He created for you mates from among yourselves, that you may dwell in tranquillity with them, and He has put love And mercy between your (hearts): Verily in that are signs for those who reflect." 30(21)

"It is made lawful for you to go unto your wives on the night of the fast. They are raiment for you and you are raiment for them. Allah is aware that you were deceiving yourselves in this respect and He has turned in mercy towards you. So hold intercourse with them and seek that which Allah has ordained for you, and eat and drink until the white thread becometh distinct to you from the black thread

of the dawn. Then strictly observe the fast till nightfall and touch them not, but be at your devotion in the mosques. These are the limits imposed by Allah, so approach them not. Thus Allah expoundeth his revelation to mankind that they may ward off (evil") 2(187)

"And those who pray, "Our Lord! Grant unto us wives and offspring who will be the comfort of our eyes, and give us (the grace) to lead the righteous." 25(74)

FAMILY RIGHTS

The head of a family has many obligations towards the family, including but not limited to love and affection, care, financial support, quality time. If one fasts during days and prays during nights and does not allow the family its rights, the person is not a true Muslim. *Mohammed (s) said an occasion, "The money you spend on your family is your best charity" (Al-Bokhari, Al-Muslim).* A Muslim scholar once said, "A night-long sleep after the whole day of hard work for the sake of earning lawful bread and butter for your family is better than all night prayer." The following references from the Hadith highlight these points.

Narrated Kaab-bin-Malik: The Prophet of Allah (s) and his companions passed by a strong man who was working. One of the companions commented, "Would not it be wonderful if this man was using his strength in the way of Allah (S) {fighting for the cause of Allah (S) in a Holy War}. The Prophet said, "If the man is working to support his parents, his children, his family, and or himself; he is using his strength in the way of Allah (S). But if the man is working just for his pride or to show of his strength, he is using his strength in the way of Satan." (Al-Tabrani)

Islam does not teach its followers to neglect, sacrifice, and give-up their family at the cost of the religion. That is why, solitary life is not recommended in Islam. Unlike many religions, Islam is a social religion and it encourages followers to socialize. Mohammed (s) once said, "Marriage is half of the faith." The life of Mohammed (s) is an open example for his followers. Mohammed (s) was a good husband, a wonderful father and grandfather, an excellent general, a unique leader, an exceptional businessman, and above all he had the duties of prophecy. He did the best job in each and every field of his life in a very beautiful way. One day he said to his companions, *"Do not chase people away from Islam by talking about the religion all the time." (AL-Bokhari)*

Mohammed (s) is a role model for the every Muslim to follow. Give quality time to your family like he did. Provide them with physical, economic, mental, moral, and spiritual support and do all this under the commandments of Allah (S), as Mohammed (s) had done. After that, seek blessings, success, and help from Allah (S). Following references from the Qur'an highlight the importance of family and family values in Islam.

"O you who believe! save yourselves and your families from a fire whose fuel is men and stones, over which are (appointed) angels stern (and) severe, who flinch not (from executing) the commands they receive from Allah, but do (precisely) what they are commanded." 66(6)

After the battle of Ohad, Jabir came to the Prophet (s) and said: "O, Prophet of Allah! I was very eager to fight in the battle of Ohad but my father prevented me from going, on the plea that there was no male member in the house to look after my seven sisters. As he had made up his mind to go, he bade me stay back with the family. He met the most coveted end (i.e. martyrdom) in Ohad. Now I am very eager to go with you this time and fight against the Qureysh." The Prophet (s) advised him to stay and look after his father's family.

Narrated Ibn-e-Omar (R): The news of my daily fasting and praying every night throughout the night reached the Prophet (s). When he met me, he said, "I have been informed that you fast every day and pray every night. Fast (for some days) and give up fasting (for some days); pray and sleep, for your eyes have a full claim on you, and your body and your family (parents, wife and children) have full claim on you." (Al-Bokhari)

Narrated Ibn-e-Omar (R): The Prophet (s) said, "All of you are guardians and are responsible for your wards. A ruler is a guardian of his peasants; a man is a guardian of his family; a lady is a guardian and is responsible for her husband's house and his offspring; and so all of you are guardian and all of you are responsible for your wards." (Al-Bokhari)

PART II

RIGHTS OF CHILDREN

COURTSHIP

Amazingly, in the present world, courtship is socially accepted among Non-Muslim cultures. Muslims, however, are divided into quite a few groups regarding dating. A so-called modern group of Muslims have chosen to follow the open dating game for themselves and for their children, which apparently seems to be hurting their inner Islam and emotion. Another extreme side of Muslims choose and enforce the mate on their children. The third group of Muslims have developed a new philosophy of dating. They permit their children to date with Muslim children only. Many so-called Islamic societies in the USA are following the same strategy and allowing Muslim children to intermix and find someone compatible among themselves. To achieve this goal, these societies arrange Islamic-camps during summer vacations. The Muslims with this believe also insist that their way is the right way. The last but not least group of Muslims arrange marriages only at the children's consent.

The first three of the above four types of Muslim-parents are wrong. First two groups are renegadors. The third group needs to improve their understanding towards Islam. In the next few lines, I would like to clarify where this group stands wrong. As Allah (S) has mentioned in the Qur'an, "***Do not go close to adultery***." This order explicitly closes all doors to dating, kissing, and hugging are any potential route to intimacy.

Note here! Had Allah (S) DID NOT say in the Qur'an, "*Do not commit adultery*." This statement could have been interpreted such that dating, kissing, and hugging are not counted as adultery so are permitted. Allah (S) knows the human mentality so He took care of the problem by using appropriate statement and left no chance for misinterpretation.

Adultery is one of the four major sins in Islam and any situation, events, circumstances, or effort that drives a person toward adultery is prohibited under this order. Severity of the situation does not change whether dating is conducted between the two Muslims, or between a Muslim and a Non-Muslim, or between two Non-Muslims. Under all circumstances, dating is as elicit as adultery. Period. To eliminate remote chances of remote adultery, Islam prohibits even brothers and sisters -who have reached the age of puberty- to be left alone in closed proximity without adult supervision.

The group that allows their children to pick one among quite a few proposals and permits them to talk and understand each other over the phone or under the supervision of adults is the best of all.

FAMILY PLANNING

The birth control issue has divided the Islamic jurisprudence into three different schools of thought. Each of which has a solid evidence from the Qur'an and the Hadith in their favor. I am going to highlight each of the three opinions and will mention my own point of view at the end.

The first school of thought takes its opinion from the Qur'an (Reference below) and does not believe in the use of any type of contraception.

"Kill not your children for fear of want: We shall provide sustenance for them as well as for you. Verily, the killing of them is a great sin." 17(31)

This group believes that Allah (S) is the ultimate Provider so no life should be protected or prevented from being born. From this point of view, use of any contraception is Un-Islamic. The second school of thought is a little bit liberal and allows the use of contraception. This group, however, does not permit abortion under any circumstance if a woman conceives. The third group of scholars agrees to the abortion if pregnancy is less than twelve weeks. Their reference also comes from a Hadith that discusses the issue that soul enters in the baby after three months of the pregnancy.

Narrated Abdullah (R): I asked the Prophet (s), "O prophet of Allah (s)! Which sin is the greatest?" He (s) said, "To ascribe partners to Allah (S).
I asked, "What next?"
He (s) said, "To kill your child fearing of poverty."
I further asked, "What next?,"
He (s) said, "To commit adultery." (Al-Bokhari)

From my point of view, all of these opinions are right and can be followed because each opinion is based on strong evidence from the Qur'an and Hadith.

GENDER

Traditionally, parents like to have a male than a female child. Some parents want to have boys to carry on the family name. Others blame western society that, they believe, is unfavorable for the upbringing of girls. Both of the above statements are untrue from my point of view. The training that parents provide for their children in their own home is what really counts. For whatever reason, parents are more liberal towards their sons than daughters. They tend not to tolerate any Un-Islamic conduct from their daughter(s), but care less if their son(s) practice the same. For example, some parents do not mind when their son(s) are very out-going but cannot stand if their daughter(s) do the same. Islamic rules and regulations should, however, be implemented equally upon men and women.

The Qur'an and the history of Islam tell us that daughters were often more obedient and caring towards parents than sons. For example, in the Qur'an, some of the sons, wives and fathers of the Prophets (As) have been described disbelievers. There is no evidence in the Qur'an, that daughters of a believer ever disobeyed parents, however. That probably was the reason, Allah (S) bestowed four daughters on Mohammed (s), His most beloved Prophet (s).

Mohammed (s) once said, "If somebody has three daughters, and he is kind to them, teaches them good manners, and treats them nicely, Allah (S) will save him from the hellfire on the day of judgment." According to another saying of Mohammed (s), "A girl is born with seven and a boy with one blessing of Allah (S)." A companion asked for an explanation and Mohammed (s) explained: "Angels make the shape of a new baby in the mother's womb. When they come to the sexual organs, they ask Allah (S) for the sex of the baby. If Allah (S) says boy, they go ahead and make male sex features. When Allah (S) says girls, angels confirm this order seven times and Allah (S) repeats it seven times before they make the female sex features of the new born baby." According to another saying of the Prophet (s), "Daughters will act as a barrier between the hellfire and the parents." (Bokhari-, Muslim)

Parents must treat their sons and daughters equally. Both boys and girls are blessings from Allah (S). Nor should parents make their daughter feel that her brother is dearer and more important to parents than her. Some parents celebrate a boy's birth and feel sad when a girl is born in their house. Many of my female students have encountered this behavior of their parents. For example, one of my female students in an Islamic Sunday School in America once told me that her parents had arranged a big feast when her younger brother was born and she witnessed her parents crying at the birth of her younger sisters. She asked me whether, in Islam, daughters were an inferior creation of Allah (S) than were sons. I would like my readers to answer this question to their own daughter(s). I, however, told the student that Islam teaches equality among all children and that the conduct of her parents was Un-Islamic. Below is a reference from the Qur'an to guide us in this regard.

" To Allah belongs the dominion of the heavens and the earth. He creates what He wishes. He bestows (children) male or female according to His wish. Or He bestows both males and females, and He leaves barren whom He will: For He is full of knowledge and power." 42(49-50)

PARENTAL WISHES

Wanting a son or praying to have a son is permissible in Islam. The Qur'an provides many examples to the readers where several Prophets of Allah (S) prayed to have a son even though they were very old and their wives were barren. This indicates that we can pray to Allah (S) for a son at any time in our lives. This is also another way of Allah (S) to teach us how to pray for a son. Allah (S) has shown that the Prophets (As), who were very near and dear to Him, prayed for a son; so should we. Moreover, today's technology is advanced enough to make a woman conceive a baby with the gender of the parents' choice. From my point of view, parents can use today's technology for this purpose. Parents however, should not go too extreme and abort the baby with unwanted gender.

"Then Zachariah prayed unto his Lord and said: My Lord! Bestow upon me a goodly offspring from your bounty. Lo! You are the hearer of prayer." 3(38)

"Now I {Zakaria (A)} fear (what) my relatives (and colleagues) (will do) after me: But my wife is barren: So give me an heir as from Yourself." 19(5)

'He {Zakariya (A)} said: "O my Lord how shall I have a son, when my wife is barren and I have grown quite decrepit from old age?"' 19(8)

'And (remember) Zakariya, when he cried to his Lord: "O my Lord! leave me not without offspring, though You are the best of inheritors."' 21(89)

'But when he {Abraham (A)} saw their hands not reaching towards the (meal), he felt some mistrust of them, and conceived a fear of them, they said: "Fear not: we have been sent against the people of Lot."
And his wife was standing (there), and she laughed: "But We gave her glad

tidings of Isaac, and after him, of Jacob.
She said: "Alas for me! shall I bear a child, seeing I am an old woman, and my husband here is an old man? That would indeed be a wonderful thing."
They said: "Don't you wonder at Allah's decree? The grace of Allah and His blessings on you, O you people of the house! For He is indeed worthy of all praise, full of all glory." 11(70-73)

'But his {Abraham's (A)} wife came forward clamoring: she smote her forehead and said: "A barren old woman!"' 51(29)

'He said: "I will go to my Lord! He will surely guide me! O my Lord! grant me a righteous (son)!" So We gave him the good news of a bearing son.' 37(99-101)

42

GRATITUDE

After the safe birth of a child, people say, "Thanks to the doctor who treated me so I could bear a child." "Thank you honey," we say to our spouse, "For giving me such a lovely child." "Thank you doctor for saving the life of our child." These and other related grateful phrases are often used by the parents around us. Did we ever spend a moment and think, Who really has given us this child, Who really has saved the life of our child, and Who really deserves our thanks besides doctors and spouse? Perhaps not. If we did, we would have realized that we have breached the rights of Creator in our above statements. Please do not quote me wrong. Expressing thanks to doctors and spouse after the birth of a child is not wrong under any circumstances. Nurses, doctors, and all others are the tools of Allah (S) and must be complimented. We should, however, always accolade Allah (S) before thanking anybody else. Instead, we should have said, "All praises are for Allah (S), the Lord of the universe, Who has given us this child or Who has saved the life of our child through wonderful people like you." Allah (S) has expressed the same concerns in the Qur'an in the following ways:

"It is He Who has created you from a single person, and made his mate of like nature, in order that he might dwell with her (in love). When they are united she bears a light burden and carries it about (unnoticed). When she grows heavy, they both pray to Allah, their Lord, (saying): "If You give us a goodly child, we vow we shall (ever) be grateful." But when He gives them a goodly child, they ascribe to others a share in the gift they have received: But Allah is exalted, high above the partners, they ascribe to Him." 7(189-190)

"Parenting in Islam" By Javed I Khan

"That it is He, Who gives wealth and satisfaction". 53(48)

MOTHER'S INSTINCTS

A thirteen-year-old boy was sleeping in his room on a stormy night when his parents were sleeping in a separate portion of the house. Suddenly the boy's mother, jumped out of her bed and ran to her son's room. She dragged the sleeping boy outside the room. Soon after the boy was dragged out of the room, the entire roof of the son's room fell down. The incident was so quick and sudden that everybody in the household was stunned. Later the mother explained her experience that she heard a whisper in her mind while asleep, "Save your son, save your son, the roof of his room is about to fall." "And I followed the instructions," she added. This is one of the many examples of mother's instinct. On many occasions during the course of raising children, mothers get special feelings about their children. These feelings come from Allah (S) as a precautionary measure to protect or to save the children from any forthcoming danger. We shall find many facts around us when many mothers have saved their children's lives just by following their instincts. Many mothers, on the other hand, have lost their children just by ignoring their instincts. Mothers, please, do not ignore these feelings.

Below is the story of the mother of Moses (A) from the Qur'an as a proof of mother's instinct. The story narrates that how she was inspired by Allah (S). Notice here, that the mother, not the father of Moses (A), was inspired by Allah (S). The father of a child, however, may or may not have the same feelings and inspiration about the children as does the mother:

"And remember, We rescued you from Pharaoh's people who afflicted you with

the worst of penalties, who slew your male children and saved alive your females: In what was a momentous trial from your Lord." 7(141)

"Truly, Pharaoh elated himself in the land and divided its people into sections, depressing a group among them: their sons he slew, but he kept alive their females: For he was indeed an evil-doer." 28(4)

"So We sent this inspiration to the mother of Moses: "Suckle (your child), but when you have fear about him, cast him into the river. But fear not, nor grieve: For We shall restore him to you, and We shall make him one of Our messengers." 28(7)

"Behold! We sent to your {Moses (A)} mother, by inspiration, the message: Place (the child) into the chest, and throw (the chest) into the river: the river will cast him up on the bank, and he will be taken up by one who is an enemy to Me and an enemy to him. But I endowed you with love from Me: And (this) in order that you may be reared under My eyes. Behold! your sister went and said, Shall I show you one who will nurse and rear the (child)? So We brought you back to your mother, that her eye might be cooled and she should not grieve." 20(38-40)

"And she (Moses' mother) said to the sister of {Moses (A)}, "Trace him". So she (the sister) watched him from a distance and they perceived not.

"Then the people of Pharaoh picked him up (from the river): (It was intended) that {Moses (A)} should be to them an adversary and a cause of sorrow: For Pharaoh and Haman and (all) their hosts were men of sin. The wife of Pharaoh said: "(Here is) a joy for the eyes, for me and for you: Slay him not. It may be that he will be of use to us, or we may adopt him as a son." And they perceived not (what they were doing).And We ordained that he refused to suck at first, until (his sister came up and) said: "Shall I point out to you the people of a house that will nourish and bring him up for you and take care of him?" And the heart of the mother of Moses became void: She was going almost to disclose his (case), had We not strengthened her heart (With faith), so that she might remain a (firm) believer. Thus did We restore him to his mother, that her eyes might be comforted, that she might not grieve, and that she might know that the promise of

Allah is true: But most of them do not know. When he reached full age, and was firmly established (in life), We bestowed on him wisdom and knowledge: for thus do We reward those who do good." 28(8-14)

BABY SITTING

Foster care was a very common practice among pre-Islamic Arabs in what is now Saudi Arabia. Rich people would sent their newborn babies away with nannies for a long period of time so their children could grow up in healthy suburban areas and could learn good etiquettes. During that time, parents would either visit their children, or nannies would bring the children to parents. History tells us that Mohammed (s) was also sent with Haleema (R), a nanny, a few days after his birth and was returned back to his mother after five years.

The parents of the Pre-Islamic era would consider the family background of nannies so they could brag in front of their competitors that their children were nursed by and raised in a superior family.

After the revelation of Islam, however, priorities in the selection of nannies/baby-sitters were changed. The first consideration for selection of a nanny for a Muslim child became a strong religious family background, secondly the economical condition, and last but not least, the social background of a nanny. To baby-sit Muslim children, nannies from a religious but poor family background got preference over a rich family. This was another way in which Islam taught his followers to help poor but worthy religious families.

Sending children to baby-sitters is currently a very common practice for working parents. I shall request that all Muslim parents who send their children to baby-sitters should follow the same consideration and criteria for the selection of a baby-sitter as were used by early Muslims. This criterion will help Muslim children to grow up in a better and more Islamic atmosphere and also help poor Muslim families to have a good source of income. Moreover, the money you spend in this regard will not only be <u>tax deductible</u>, it will also be counted as your charity in the eyes of Allah (S).

ROLE MODELS

Starting from the cradle, human being has a tendency and urge to pick a role model. This changes with the age, understanding, maturity, and mental development. Fortunately- parents have the advantage to be the first role models for every child of their own, and a home is the first little world a child experiences. Each and every aspect of parents' daily life is being studied, admired, and copied by child(ren) of the house. This includes -but is not restricted to- the physical setting of a house, action and interaction between spouses, parents, friends, and neighbors. If children are exposed to a good, religious, productive, caring, and educated home life, they will learn to value these things NOT otherwise.

A friend of mine, saw the following note posted in the room of his friend's son:

> Rule # 1. Dad is always wrong.
> Rule # 2. If you think Dad is right, refer to the rule number one.

Because the rules in that household were made for children only adults were exempt from the rules. Allah (S) has mentioned this concern in following Ayah of the Qur'an.

> *"O you who believe! Why do you say that which you do not do? Grievously odious is it in the sight of Allah that you say which you do not do." 61(2-3)*

"Parenting in Islam" By Javed I Khan

 <u>Unfortunately</u>, being a role model comes with the responsibility. It is tough and it requires constant efforts from the role model part to keep up the image and stay steady in front of the followers. For example, smoking parents as a role model have no right to forbid their children from smoking. Some say, "Well we do not smoke in front of children, so we can give them lectures against smoking." Remember this is a hypocritical behavior and worse happens when children learn about the other side of the their role models. Every parent thinks that lying is a bad habit. No parent wants his/her children to develop this habit. Sometime parents may teach their children to lie without realizing it. For instance, a child wants parents to attend a sport event at school with him on a working day. The Parent call in sick from work in front of the child and go the attend the spots event. Or a parent may not want to answer a phone call and asks child to answer and tell the caller that "DAD or MOM" is not home. When children are permitted to lie on parents' behalf, they have right to lie for themselves as well.

 If parents do not want children to steal, they must not practice dishonesty in front of them. For example, one day a father saw his child with a pencil that he did not remember buying. Further investigation led him to the fact that the child had stolen the pencil from a classmate. The father got angry at the child for stealing a pencil and advised him, "Do not ever steal because stealing is bad. Whenever you need a pencil, let me know and I will get you one from my office." The child knows that his father works for somebody in that office. Following is a story from the real role model of the Muslims:

A lady brought her five-year-old son to Mohammed (s) and said, "O Prophet of

*Allah (S), my son eats lots of sweet stuff, please forbid him from that."
Mohammed (s) told the mother to bring her son back in a couple of days. A
couple of days latter, the lady returned with the son. This time Mohammed (s)
brought the boy close, hugged and kissed him, then advised him not to eat that
much sweet stuff. The surprised mother asked Mohammed (s) that he could have
advised the same to the boy when she brought him the first time and so could have
saved her a trip. The Prophet replied, "Because "I had just finished eating a lot of
sweet stuff just before you came that day, so I did not want to advise him. I
preach what I practice. I have not eaten any of the sweet stuff since that day in
order to advise your son." (Ibn-e-Daud)*

Do not expect children to go and read their textbooks in a
corner of the house where parents are watching a television show.
If parents want children to read, they should read with them as
well. Set a schedule for the entire family in your daily routine for
study, television, homework, play, prayer etc. This way teaches
children that everybody in the home values the same things.
Practice what you preach is the only way your children will follow
your instructions willingly. The key is this: Do what you want them
to do, act how you want them to act, and behave the way you want
them to behave. Otherwise, your children shall stop listening to you
and will not take your advice seriously. They shall consider you,
rightly, a hypocrite and shall not respect you.

Creating a healthy atmosphere for our children is our job.
How their personality develops, however, is in the hands of Allah
(S), Who manages to create the right kind of atmosphere for a child
by His mysterious ways. That's why, sometimes, devils come from
the house of saints and saints from the house of Satan. For
example, Moses (A) was brought up in the house of Pharaoh and
Noah's son was raised in the house of a Prophet (A)

EXPLORING AGE

Allah (S) has bestowed a unique nature to each and every individual. That nature leads individuals to play a certain role and act accordingly in the society during the course their lives. Which is why, nature dominates over the man-made atmosphere around individuals right from childhood. As a result, children tend to develop their natural behavior at an early age. For instance, Abraham (A) and Mohammed (s) had rejected the false atmosphere that was created around them by their parents, family members, society. As we know, both of them were born in the middle of idol worshipers, yet both refused the ideology of their forefathers. Let us look into the Qur'an to find out more in this respect:

"When Abraham said to his father, Azar: "When you take idols for gods, I see you and your folk in error manifest." So also did We show Abraham the Kingdom of the heavens and the earth that he might have certitude. When night grew dark upon him he beheld a star. He said: This is my lord. But when it set, he said: I love not the things that set. And when he saw the moon uprising, he exclaimed: This is my lord. But when it set, he said: Unless my Lord guide me, I surely become one of the folk who are astray. And when he saw the sun uprising, he cried: This is my lord! This is greater! And when it is set he exclaimed: O my people! I am free from all that you associate (with Him)". 6(74-78)

Guidance is not a process of pushing or a pulling, it is rather motivation and exploration. For example, Allah (S) could have created all human being alike with Goodness and straightforwardness. He could have evenly distributed the wealth among them. But He did not, because this is against His nature. His ways of Guidance are hidden in search and exploration. So the natural method for the guidance lies in flowing along the stream of the children's dynamic rather than going against it. For example, one of my childhood friends was a genius in mathematics and engineering. He was so intelligent that he would pull a car's engine apart and would reassemble in a few hours without any assistance when he was just thirteen years old. Unfortunately, he was born in to a family of doctors. His parents, grandparents, uncles, and aunts were doctors, so his father insisted that he MUST study medicine with no second choice. My friend failed biology class numerous times because he could not comprehend biology and later quit school with disappointment. He is now a car mechanic. Forcing children against their dynamic is like leading a camel. It is a slow, tiring and, sometimes heart-breaking process. In this case children are dragged into an unseen and unwanted situation. Following children's dynamic, on the other hand, is like riding a horse. This is a fast, efficient, and convenient. In this case, the children are allowed to explore their passion under the true paternal guidance.

LISTENING TO CHILDREN

I grew up in a society where children's participation in adult conversation is considered rude, disrespectful, and Un-Islamic. This is incorrect. Children deserve to participation in any discussion as much as other adults do. Listening to children's needs, viewpoints, and desires, is a part and parcel of parenting. Many child-psychologists have recommended that the children should be encouraged and brought into the adults' conversation. Ere I mean a good and constructive discussion. It is the inception of children's self-esteem, power of communication, general knowledge, ways of expression, and vocabulary. This approach also helps to recognize the inner-potential of children.

Parents must listen to children very carefully. Never ignore their feedback on any issue. If their feedback does not make any sense, guide them accordingly. Give some serious thoughts before completely rejecting their thoughts just because their youth and inexperience. If their conversation makes sense, accept it without hesitation without making it any threat to your ego. Allah (S) might have bestowed more insight or understanding upon your children than on you and their observations might have been gifted from Allah (S). Allah (S) wants to make us understand the same concept in the following part of the Qur'an.

"That is Our argument. We gave it unto Abraham against his folk. We raise unto degrees of wisdom whom We will. lo! the Lord is Wise, Aware." 6(80)

"When he reached full age, and was firmly established (in life), We bestowed on him wisdom and knowledge: for thus do We reward those who do good." 28(14)

55

"O my father! I have received knowledge which has not reached you: so follow me: I shall guide you to a way that is even and straight." 19(43)

Below is the story of Abraham's (A) childhood. This story is narrated in the Qur'an. Abraham (A) was a gifted child but his father did not recognize this gift due to his false pride and stubbornness. Over and over, Abraham (A) shared his observations with his father and tried to convince him, but the father did not listen. The father probably felt that following his son's advice would bring him embarrassment and shame from friends, family, and society.

'Behold, he {Abraham (A)} said to his father: "O my father! why do you worship that which can neither hear nor see, and neither can profit you? "O my father! I have received knowledge which has not reached you: so follow me: I shall guide you to a way that is even and straight. "O my father! serve not Satan: for Satan is a rebel against (Allah) most Gracious. "O my father! I fear lest a chastisement afflict you from (Allah) most Gracious, so that you become to Satan a friend." (The father) replied, "Are you shrinking from my gods, O Abraham? If you forbear not, I will indeed stone you: Now get away from me for a good long while." Abraham said: "Peace be on you: I will pray to my Lord for your forgiveness: For He is the Most Gracious to me. "And I will turn away from you (all) and from those whom you invoke besides Allah: I will call on my Lord perhaps; by my prayer to my Lord, I shall be blessed."' 19(42-48)

'Behold! Abraham said to his father and his people: "I do indeed clear myself of what you worship: "(I worship) only him Who originated me, and He will certainly guide me." '43(26-27)

'Behold! he {Abraham (A)} said to his father and his people, "What are these images, to which you are (so assiduously) devoted?" They said, "We found our fathers worshipping them." He said, "Indeed you and your fathers have been in manifest error." They said, "Have you brought us the truth, or are you one of those who jest?" He said, "Nay, your Lord is the Lord of the heavens and the

earth, he who created them (from nothing): and I am a witness to this (truth). "And by Allah, I will certainly plan against your idols after you go away and turn your backs."
So he broke them to pieces, (all) but the biggest of them, that they might turn (and address themselves) to it. They said, "Who has done this to our gods? He must indeed be one of the unjust one. They said, "We heard a youth talk of them: He is called Abraham."' 21(52-60)

'Behold, he {Abraham (A)} said to his father and his people: "What worship you?" They said: "We worship idols, and we remain constantly in attendance on them."' 26(70-71)
"Behold, he said to his father and to his people, "What is that which you worship? "Is it a falsehood-god other than Allah that you desire?" "Then what is your idea About the Lord of the Worlds? Then did he cast a glance at the stars, And he said, "I am Indeed sick (at heart)!" So they turned away from him, and departed. Then did he turn to their gods and said, "Will you not eat (Of the offerings before you)? "What is the matter with you that you speak not?" Then did he turn upon them, striking (them) with the right hand. Then came (the worshippers) with hurried steps, to him.
He said: "Worship you that which you have (Yourselves) carved? "But Allah has created you and your handiwork! They said, "Build him a furnace, and throw him into the blazing fire." (This failing), they then Plotted against him, but We made them the ones most humiliated." 37(85-98)

"Here is an excellent example for you to follow Abraham and those with him, when they said to their people, "We are clear of you and of whatever you worship besides Allah: we have rejected you, and there has arisen, between us and you, enmity and hatred for ever, unless you believe in Allah And Him alone": But not when Abraham said to his father: "I will pray for forgiveness for you, though I have no power (to get) ought on your behalf from Allah." (They prayed): "Our Lord! in You do we trust, and to You do we turn in repentance: to You is (our) final return." 60(4)

Children who ask more questions learn faster. They might be more intelligent than children who ask fewer questions or who do not ask any questions. Never discourage your children from asking questions, pay undivided heed to what they say, answer the questions carefully, correctly, appropriately, and from the best of your knowledge. Parents should not answer any questions beyond their own knowledge, however. Acknowledge the limit of your knowledge. Never give them wrong answers for their temporary satisfaction. Because children take everything you say literally, your wrong answers might mislead them forever. Guide them to the right source of knowledge, instead.

Do not answer their questions with a small gesture or simply with "Yes" or "No" answers.. Answer the questions with some logical reasons and examples. For example, your child wants to see Allah (S). Do not tell your child that (s)he cannot see Allah (S). Instead, tell him/her that Allah (S) can be seen- indirectly- through His evidence and that our eyes are incapable of seeing Allah (S) in this world. Refer him/her to the Qur'anic dialogues between Moses (A) and Allah (S). In which Moses (A) wanted to see Allah (S) and Allah (S) replied, "You cannot see Me." Then show your child some of the mighty creations of Allah (S), such as the sun, the moon, and the stars and explain to him/her that NONE but Allah (S) has power to create these objects.

DETERRING CHILDREN

Another responsibility of parents is to deter and prepare children from any danger that could potentially come from a natural or a manmade source with the hurtful intention. Children should also be made aware of potential dangerous situations? What should the children do when they encounter a dangerous situation (other then calling 911 in the USA or 15 in Pakistan)? For example parent should prepare action, escape, and survival plan for disasters like earthquake, fire, burglary, and robbery.

Children should be told that who should and who should not be trusted and why should they trust somebody and not everybody. For example, if you want to forbid your child from interacting with a neighbor across the street who uses bad language, tell the child that (s)he should not interact with the people who use bad language. This is an indirect way of telling the child that (s)he should stay away from the neighbor across the street. A constructive approach should be used while conveying such information to children.

Below is the story of Yousuf (A), whose father, Yaqoob (A), informed him about expected dangers from Yousuf's step-brothers. The information was delivered to Yousuf (A) in a very careful and beautiful way. Yaqoob (A) did not use any bad words or foul language against his sons, yet he warned Yousuf(A) in a very protective way that his step-brothers were not his well-wishers.

'Behold: Yousuf said to his father, "O my father! I did see eleven stars and the sun and the moon: I saw them prostrating themselves onto me!" Said the father, "My (dear) little son! do not tell your vision to your (step) brothers, they might not plot a plot against you: Since Satan is for man an open enemy!"' 12(4-5)

"Parenting in Islam" By Javed I Khan

In early Islamic days, parents used to teach free-style wrestling to children as a tool of self-defense or survival. Martial art, such as Karate, is the present day's "wrestling" which builds up confidence and self-esteem in children. I shall encourage parents to put their children (boys and girls) in a Karate school so they could learn to defend themselves in critical circumstances.

GUIDING CHILDREN

Irrespective of race, religion, creed, color, origin, and family background; no parent wants his or her children to lie, steal, cheat, or otherwise misbehave. Islamic teachings have the same concerns. Make your intention Islamic, when teaching moral values to children. For instance- sharing, bearing good moral character, respecting elders and loving younger, being nice, helping needy and visiting sick people are the qualities every parent wants to see in their children. These and many other good qualities that we want our children to possess could be rewarding for us if we convey to them with the Islamic intention. That is how we shall benefit from everything we do here in this life and in the life hereafter. Use the guideline that has been mentioned in the Qur'an on many occasions:

'The same did Abraham enjoin upon his sons, and also Jacob, (saying): "O my sons! Lo! Allah has chosen for you the true religion; therefore die not except as men who have surrendered (unto Him)." Or were you present (O Mohammed) when death came to Jacob, when he said on to his sons: "What will you worship after me?" they said: "We shall worship your God, The God of your father Abraham and Isaac, One God, and onto Him we have surrendered."' 2(132-133)

"Behold, Luqman said to his son, admonishing him, "O my son! Join not in worship (others) with Allah: for false worship is indeed the highest wrong-doing." 31(13)
But He fashioned him in due proportion, and breathed into him of His spirit. And He gave you (the faculties of) hearing and sight and understanding. Little thanks do you give!" 32(9)

"Parenting in Islam" By Javed I Khan

ADVISING CHILDREN

The use of practical approach when advising children is important. For example, if your teenage child smokes, do not punish him or stop him directly. Instead, take him to a nearest cancer center and show him people who are suffering from lung cancer and tell him the cause of the disease. If your teenage child drinks alcohol, take him to a cancer center and show him people who are suffering from liver cancer and tell him the cause of their suffering. Display large colored posters of healthy and carcinogenic lungs or liver in or around his room. Also inform him that Allah (S) loves us like an artist loves his created art and He wants us to live a healthy live. Allah (S) does not want his creation to hurt them so he forbade them from indulgence in hurtful activities.

The Qur'an has also guided us in how to advise our children by providing us appropriate phrases which tell us how, when, and what to say for given circumstances. These phrases are applicable to all people that indicate that Islam is the religion for mankind.

"But if they strive to make you join in worship with Me things of which you have no knowledge, obey them not: yet bear them company in this life with justice (And consideration), and follow the way of those who turn to Me: In the end, the return of you all is to Me. And I will tell you all that you did." O my son!" {said Luqman (A) to his son}, "If there be (but) the weight of a mustard-seed and it were (hidden) in a rock, or (anywhere) in the heavens or on earth, Allah will bring it forth: for Allah is subtle and aware." "O my son! establish regular prayer, enjoin what is just, and forbid what is wrong: and bear with patient constancy whatever betides you; for this is firmness (of purpose) in (the conduct of) affairs. "And swell not your cheek (for pride) at men. Nor walk in insolence through the earth: for Allah loves not any arrogant boaster. "And be moderate in your pace, and lower your voice; for the harshest of sounds without doubt is the braying of the ass." Do

you not see that Allah has subjected to your (use) all things in the heavens and on earth, and has made His bounties flow to you in exceeding measure, (both) seen and unseen? Yet there are among men those who dispute about Allah, without knowledge and without guidance, and without a book to enlighten them. When they are told to follow the (revelation) that Allah has sent down, they say: "No, we shall follow the ways that we found our fathers (following)." What! even if it is satin beckoning them to the chastisement of the (blazing) fire? Whoever submits his whole self to Allah, and is a doer of good, has grasped indeed the firmest hand-hold: and to Allah shall all things return." 31(15-22)

SACRIFICING FOR CHILDREN

Many child psychologists have proven in their research that the children who were raised by single or divorced parents generally develop certain personality disorders. Others types of personality disorders were also observed in the children whose parents always fought with each other. Astonishingly, children who lived with single parent with one deceased parent did not show any abnormality in their behavior. Also, no personality disorder was observed in the children who were living with both loving parents. These children were mentally, emotionally, spiritually, and physically strong and healthy. They receive very good test scores and their behavior, attitude, and aptitude were found to be very pleasant.

Eventhough they do not or cannot say anything to their splitting parents, children are affected the most from parental divorce. According to child psychologists, divorce is like a saw that rips children's souls into pieces. Fourteen hundred years ago when there was no concept of child psychology, *Mohammed (s)* mentioned, *"Divorce is the most hideous act in the eyes of Allah (S), Who has permitted it as a last resort for convenience of mankind."* So from the Islamic point of view, divorce is allowed as a last resort for married couples. This means is the last options after everything like communication, understanding, relationships, sacrifices, compromises, patience, and agreements have failed. This is the reason that the divorce rate in Muslim communities is much less.

The divorce rate among the Muslim communities living in the bright side of the world, however, is growing rapidly as compared to the Muslims living in Muslim countries. This rapid rise reminds us that the Muslims are losing their Islamic values by following the Non-Muslims. For those parents, I have a suggestion: Before you even think of divorcing your spouse, look into the eyes of your innocent children and read the message from their tearful eyes. Put your heart in their little body and ask yourself, what would you have thought if your parents were splitting apart? After getting these answers from yourself, go ahead and do what you think is right.

Old age is considered the most unfortunate age in the bright part of the world. Nobody seems to feel any empathy toward elderly individuals. Their old age becomes miserable and lonely that ends in nursing homes. The reason is very obvious, simple, and understandable. When today's old generation was strong, in-control and healthy yesterday, they acted selfishly toward their children. They divorced their spouses without any consideration for children. Now the tables have turned toward children side that are strong, in-control and healthy. So the children treat their parents accordingly.

CHILDREN IN MOSQUES

It was not to my surprise, when my seven-year-old son refused to go to Mosques with me in America. He told me that people in Mosques act mean towards him. This is not just my story, this is the story of every Muslim parent whose young children do not want to accompany them in Mosques. Hardly any children can be seen with parents during five-time regular praying hours; a few parents bring their children during Friday's prayers, and some during Eid's congregational prayers.

Mosques are supposed to be the place of worship and respect. Running around and making noise in the area of worship is considered to be disrespectful. Children run around and make noise in Mosques that distracts worshippers during prayers. So worshippers give mean look to children. The worshippers reprimand children on this account and make them feel that they have committed some major sin in the Mosque. Consequently, adults' ill behavior discourages children from coming to Mosques. The sense of being unwelcome in Mosques chases the children away from the Mosque forever starting very early age. Consequently they do not come to Mosques for the rest of life.

I do not have any doubts about respecting Mosques and watching our demeanors when in Mosques. These measures, however, are for obligatory for adults to follow. Many people think that children should and must act like adults when in Mosques. That is impossible. Remember: neither am I condoning children's behavior nor am I encouraging parents to let their children go wild during congregation in Mosques. All I am saying is no matter what adults say or do, children will behave as children in Mosques. Just do not give them mean look or confront them out loud. Instead, inform them about etiquettes of Mosques in a loving way because language of love is the best-understood language among children. I have seen politically opponent groups yelling, screaming, and shedding each other blood in Mosques to gain a political power. What happens to adults' demeanor at that time?

In my opinion, take children to Mosques, let them run around, let them make noise, and let them distract your attention from the prayers. Potentially, children are watching their parents and elders praying. Internally, they are developing a habit of coming to the house of Allah (S). Psychologically, they are preparing themselves for tomorrow to stand in the rows and pray to Allah (S) beside their parents. Neither should you discourage parents from bringing their children to Mosques, nor should you impose any unwanted discipline on the children in Mosques. That could potentially stop them from coming to the Mosque. It is, however, the responsibility of parents and other worshipers to motivate children so they could learn to respect the boundaries of Mosques.

Many examples are found in the life of Mohammed (s) and from the History of Islam. Children of that time were no different than today's children. Neither children nor parents were discouraged by Mohammed (s) to come to the Mosque. For example, on one occasion, Mohammed (s) was delivering a Friday sermon on the pulpit of the Mosque when his grandson, Hassan (R) (then three-year-old) was running around in the Mosque. Hassan (R) suddenly tripped and fell on the floor of the Mosque and started crying. Mohammed (s) discontinued his sermon, went and picked up and pampered Hassan (R), did not resume his sermon until Hassan calmed down. This was the training that made Hassan (R) and Hussain (A) very distinctive individuals in the History of Islam.

DECISION MAKING

Some parents are very strict autocrats for children matters. Children are the last people to be involved in any family decision-making processes. Parents always use the benefit of their prior experiences to justify their influence over the decision-making power of children. So for so, the decision, that may have any direct impact on children are generally made by parents. Many parents live their dreams through children. This behavior of parents is un-Islamic. If it has a potential impact the decision should be with parental input. However, it is the responsibility of parents to determine if their children are capable of making the right decision or not. I mean, children must possess right decision-making abilities and prove to parents as well. Moreover, parents are also obligated to inform their children of the consequences of the decision they are planning to make. At any stage of life, however, parents should not under-estimate the potential of their children without a good reason. Lack of decision-making skills alone is enough to make children mentally weak, dependent, and deprived of self-confidence.

Islam has given us a very clear example in letting our children make their own decisions in important situations. For example, the Qur'an has told us that Abraham (A) was ordered by Allah (S) to sacrifice his son Ismail (A). It was a divine order and the father could have obeyed it without asking his son-Ismail, who was a little boy at the time. Because the order of Allah (S) was pertaining to the son, the father gave his son a choice. In other words, Allah (S) gave freedom of choice even to a child. If the divine order -which we believe must be obeyed without hesitation-has to be approved by a little child involved, so should the decision making for worldly affairs be similarly approved by the child involved. The following reference from the Qur'an agrees with my above statement.

'Then, when (the son) reached (the age of serious) work with him, He said: "O my son! I have seen in a dream that I offer you in sacrifice: now see what is your view!" (The son) said: "O my father! do as you are commanded: You will find me, if Allah so wills, one of the steadfast."
"So when they had both submitted (to Allah), and he had laid him prostrate on his forehead (for sacrifice), We called out to him, "O Abraham! "You have already fulfilled The dream!" Thus indeed do We reward Those who do right. For this was a clear trial and We ransomed him with a momentous sacrifice: And We left for him among generations (to come) in later times: "Peace and salutation to Abraham!"' 37(102- 109)

PLAYING WITH CHILDREN

Unfriendly interaction of the parents with children creates a distance between the two. The distance grows longer with age. Growing apart from each other leads to become strangers for each other. Consequently, many angles of the children's life remain hidden from parents. This distance is injurious for the parent-child relationships.

In this age, parents are overwhelmed in worldly affairs. So they have developed a quick fix for the problem. After picking them up from school, many so-called concern parents have a habit of asking study-related questions. In response to their query, parents usually get brief answers, such as, "JUST FINE," "YES," "NO," etc. This might lead the parents to believe that, "All is well." The parents might think that they have done their job as the most concerned parents. Those parents are living in a fools' paradise. It is advised not to ask these questions at that time. Parents should, rather, talk with children about something refreshing, such as light jokes, news, or some other interesting topics.

In the event, children have something special to say right after school, they shall tell on their own. Questions and answers are a part of the classroom dialogues between teachers and students. Interrogating children after six long hours of school day is like recreating the same atmosphere outside the school. This repeated situation might make them sick and tired of school, books, and study. Which, ultimately, could turn them off from school. Once children are turned off, steering them back on the right track could be tough.

"Parenting in Islam" By Javed I Khan

Usually, children discuss the issues of concern among their peers and playmates while playing. Similarly, children will express their honest school and study related opinion to parents when friendly environment is created. Spending a good portion of your time in playing with them create such an environment.

Not only, child psychologists recommend playing with children, it is also a Sunnah of Mohammed (s). Who frequently played with his grandsons, Hassan (R) and Husain (R). When the Prophet (s) used to prostrate during prayer, both grandsons would climb over his back. As a result, Mohammed (s) would prolong his prostration until the grandchildren got off of his back. Below are the references in which we see Mohammed (s) played with his grandsons and other small children.

Narrated Omar bin Khattab: Once I visited the Prophet (s) in his home. I saw him bowing on his knees and hands and Hassan bin Ali (R) was riding on his back. I said to Hassan (R), "Hassan (R)! you got a wonderful ride." The Prophet (s) answered to my remark saying, "The rider is a wonderful person, too." (Al-Bokhari)(Al-Muslim)
Narrated Ali (R) and many companions of the Prophet (s): Whenever the Prophet (s) used to hear a little child crying during the course of prayer, he used to speed up the prayer. (Al-Bokhari)(Al-Muslim)

Narrated Mohammed bin Rabia (R): When I was a boy of five, I remember, the Prophet (s) took some water from a bucket with his mouth and threw it on my face. (Al-Bokhari)
Narrated Aisha (R), the mother of faithful believers: a child was brought to the Prophet (s) and it urinated on the Prophet's clothes (s). The Prophet (s) asked for water and poured it over the soiled place {(to make it usable for prayer) and he did not change his clothes for that reason}. (Al-Bokhari)

RESPECTING CHILDREN

Respecting children and their needs is another important role of parents. Show respect for children and talk nicely about them in front of friends and family members. Do not hit, hurt, or humiliate them in front of others. Listen to them very carefully when they talk to you. Pay attention to them when they need it. Give them and their opinions importance in family matters. Also, do not compare their talent with somebody else's children.

Remember, respecting your children does not mean bragging about them or their talent or lying about their achievements. For example, if your children aren't very good in their studies, do not portray them as gifted students to your friends and family. This will not only prove you are a liar in front of your children, but also in front of your friends and family. Instead, highlight their real qualities. For example, if one of your children is a good sportsman and another is a good science student, tell your friends and family about their real talents.

Do not ignore their weakness either. Work with them on their weak-point in private. For example, if one is not doing well in mathematics and another is not very good in chemistry, work with them independently and try to figure out the root cause of the problem(s). Meet with the respective teachers and, if possible, meet with their classmates to find out if they are having the same problem. Look for one or more possible solution(s). Also, do not tease them from their weak-points, alone or in front of others. Moreover, do not use words like stupid, dumb, or fool to describe their apparent weaknesses. Instead, try different approaches and encourage their efforts of improvement. For example, if your child gets a "C" in social science and an "A" in physics, tell him/her that (s)he has abilities to prove his/her talent in social science as (s)he did in physics.

Do not hide your children's weak-points from your spouse. Always discuss their problem with each other and come up with a better solution together. Generally speaking, mothers have a tendency to hide children's weaknesses from fathers when they fear the fathers' anger. That's how some mothers may spoil their children. The father usually finds out the problem when it is too late to solve. The following Hadith shows that Mohammed (s) always spoke high of his grandchildren:

One day the prophet was delivering a Friday sermon in the mosque and Hassan (R) was playing with the Prophet's clothes. Suddenly, little Hassan (R) fell down and started crying. The Prophet (s) stopped the sermon to pick up Hassan (R) and did not continue his sermon until Hassan (R) calmed down. (Al-Bokhari)

Narrated Abu Bakara (R): I heard the Prophet(s) talking at the pulpit while Hassan (R) was sitting beside him, and one time he (s) was looking at the people and at another time looking at Hassan (R), and saying, "This son of mine is a Syed (Chief) and perhaps Allah (S) will bring about an agreement (peace) between two groups of the Muslims through him (R)." (Al-Bokhari)

Narrated Osama Bin Zaid (R) that the Prophet (s) used to put him and Hassan (R) in his (s) lap, and used to say, "O Allah! I love them so please You love them," or said something similar. (Al-Bokhari)

Narrated Omar bin Khattab: Once I visited the Prophet (s) in his (s) home. I saw him bowing on his knees and hands and Hassan bin Ali (R) was riding on his back. I said to Hassan (R), "Hassan (R)! you got a wonderful ride." The Prophet (s) replied to that remark and said, "The rider is a wonderful person too." (Al-Bokhari)(Al-Muslim)

Narrated Al Bara (R): I saw the Prophet (s) carrying Hassan (R) on his shoulder and saying, "O Allah I love him, so please You (S) love him too." (Al-Bokhari)

Narrated Ibn Abi Nu'm that he had heard Ibn-e-Omar (R) saying that the Prophet

(s) said, "Hassan (R) and Hussain (R) are my two sweet basil in this world." (Al-Bokhari)

ADORING OTHER CHILDREN

Praising their own and condemning everybody else's children is another bad habit of today's parents. Parents always try to find flaws in other's children that makes them feel good about their own children. Remember: we all are human beings and our children are not perfect. If other's children are born with some weaknesses, so do ours. Generally, we try to overlook our children's limits by pinpointing problems in other's children. As a result, we criticize other's children and they do the same with ours. In addition, to respecting our children, Islam teaches us to show kindness and respect for other's children as well. Mohammed (s) practiced it and has recommended the same for his followers.

Narrated Ibn-e-Abbas (R): When the Prophet (s) arrived at Mecca (At the time of the conquest of Mecca), the children of Bani Abdul Muttalib received him. He then mounted one of them in front and one behind his back on his horse. (Al-Bokhari)

Narrated Sa'id: Omm-e-Khalid bint Khalid bin Sa'id: My father took me to the Prophet (s) when I was a little girl, I was wearing a sharp yellow shirt. The Prophet (s) saw me and said, "Sanna, Sanna (beautiful, beautiful)." Then I started playing with the seal of his prophet-hood. My father wanted to stop me but the Prophet (s) said to my father, "Leave her alone (let her play with me)." (Al-Bokhari)

Narrated Abu Qatada (R): Once the Prophet (s) visited our home and Umamah (R) the daughter of Abi- Al-Aas was sitting on his one shoulder. He prayed in our home and when he wanted to bow (for rakoh and sajoh) he used to put her down and picked her up again when used to stand up (for Iqama). (Al-Bokhari)

Narrated Osama bin Zaid (R): The prophet of Allah (s) used to put me and

Hassan bin Ali in his lap, hug us, and used to say, O Allah (S)! I am merciful to them and asking for your mercy on them. (Al-Bokhari)

Whenever Uns bin Malik (R) used to pass by a group of boys playing, he used to greet them and used to say, "The Prophet (s) used to do so." (Al-Bokhari)

One night the Caliph Omar (R) heard baby's cry coming out of a house. So he went and knocked at the door and inquired about the reason for the crying. The mother, who did not know that she was talking with Omar (R), said, "You know our caliph, Omar (R), has announced that he would grant a bonus to every child who is not being nursed. To get the bonus, I am forcing my baby to quit drinking my milk and the baby does not like bottled milk, so he is hungry and crying." The next day Omar (R) announced that every new-born would be entitled to the bonus. (Al-Farooq)

SIBLING RIVALRY

Parent may be responsible for creating sibling rivalry among children by favoritism. Some parents may develop more love for one child than another. Perhaps this is due to one or more of the following reasons: the child looks or acts more like them, the child is very obedient, the child is very intelligent, the child is very loving or understanding, and so on. Regardless of reasons for favoritism, the parents unloved or rejected child feels hurt and jealous. This jealousy and hurt may affect the neglected child's normal mental, psychological, and physical growth. This could make the unloved child hateful and resentful towards the parents and towards the parents' favorite child.

If both parents love one child more than the rest, the other sibling feel rejected. They might try to get parents' attention in destructive ways, such as by breaking something the parents like, or by being disobedient, or by turning against parents' favorite child, or by shouting and screaming if the parents like a quiet atmosphere. Below is the story of Yousuf's stepbrothers. They felt that their father loved Yousuf (A) more than he loved them. So, they decided to get rid of their brother to attract father's love.

'Verily in Yousuf and his brothers are signs for seekers. They said, "Truly Yousuf and his brother are loved more by our father than we: But we are goodly boys! Really, our father is obviously wandering (in his mind)!" "You kill Yousuf and cast him out to some unknown land, so the favor of father may be given to you alone: For you to be righteous after that!" Said one of them: "Do not kill Yousuf, but if you must, do something, throw him down to the bottom of the well: He will be picked up by some caravan of travellers." They said: "O our father! Why do not you trust us with Yousuf, seeing we are indeed his well-wishers? "Send him with us tomorrow to enjoy himself and play and we shall take every good care of him."' 12(7-11)

"Parenting in Islam" By Javed I Khan

Sometimes a father might love one child and the mother another. If they have more than two children, the remaining siblings feel neglected. Mother's favorite child may get resentful towards the father when he or she sees the mother paying any attention to her spouse. This may lead the mother's favorite child to develop a disliking towards his or her father. Sometime spouses get on each other's nerve when they feel that his/her favorite child is not getting enough attention from the other spouse. That could lead to big spousal confrontation, separation, or even divorce.

In all of the above situations, neither the favored nor the rejected child benefits. The children develop different psychological or emotional issues that does not allow them to assimilate in the "norm" of the society. Consequently, they may fail to handle the "real" world.

If you want to raise emotionally healthy, happy, caring, and loving children, treat them equally. On a special occasion for one child, such as a birthday or graduation day, make it a special occasion for the entire family. This treatment would develop a sense of unity among the family members by demonstrating that the occasion is not for an individual but for the entire family. Always buy them gifts within the same price range. Pay equal attention to all of your children even when you seem to get along better with one. The Hadith below is very clear about treating all of your children equally.

Narrated Amir: I heard Nu'man Bin Bashir (R) on the pulpit saying, "My father gave me a gift, but my mother said that she would not agree to it unless my father made the Prophet (s) as a witness to it. So my father went to the Prophet (s) and said, 'O messenger of Allah (s)! I want to give a gift to my this son (Ibn-Bashir) but my wife wanted me to make you a witness to it.' The Prophet (s) asked, 'Have you given (the like of it) to each of your all children?' My father replied in the negative. The Prophet (s) then said, 'Be afraid of Allah(S), and be just among your children. Do not make me witness for UN-justice. Either give gifts to all your children or do not give them at all.' My father then returned and took back his gift from me." (Al-Bokhari)

RESPECTING ELDERS

A friend of mine would ask his son to imitate some elder family members and then the parents would laugh at the child's performance. Now the child is makes fun not only of every elder around but his parents as well. Had the parents stopped the child insulting elders in the very beginning, he would have learned to respect all elders, including his own parents. Teaching children to respect elders is also a part of Islam. If you want your children to respect you, show them your respect for elders so they could learn to respect their elders.

Never introduce your children to friends of your age by their first names, but by the most suitable relationship to them. For example, when you are introducing your friends to your children, introduce them as an aunt or uncle of the children rather than by the friends' first names alone. When you are introducing your friend's children who are a few years older or younger than your own children, introduce them by the appropriate relation, such as elder or younger brothers or sisters, or cousin. These values can bring about a sense of connection between young, old, and friends in the children's personalities. Islam teaches us the same thing.

Narrated Abu Huraira (R): The Prophet said, "The younger person should greet (respect) the older one, and the walking person should greet the sitting one, and the smaller number of people should greet the large number of people." (Al-Bokhari)

SHOWING LOVE AND AFFECTION

Mohammed (s) loved children and he expressed his conviction that his followers would be distinguished from others by their kindness towards children (Al-Jaffery). Feeling love for children and showing love are two completely separate things. Some parents love their children but never expressed loving feeling to children, which is incorrect. Do not let a day go by without saying and doing loving things to your children. Kissing, hugging, loving, and saying and reiterating the phrase, "I love you," many times a day, are as important as food, air, and sleep for children's normal growth and health. It costs nothing yet it makes children feel special, proud, secure, and happy. This is a part of Islam, an the Sunnah of Mohammed (s).

Narrated Abu Huraira (R): The Messenger of Allah (s) kissed Hassan and Hussain bin Ali while Aqra bin Habis-Al-Tamim was sitting beside him. Al Aqra said to the Prophet (s), "I have ten children and I have never kissed any one of them." The Prophet (s) looked at him and said, "Whoever is not merciful (to children) does not deserve mercy {of Allah (S)}." (Al-Bokhari)

Narrated Aisha (R): A bedouin came to the Prophet (s) and said, "I have seen you kissing your boys (children and grandchildren)! we do not kiss ours." The Prophet said, "I cannot put mercy in your heart after Allah (S) has taken the mercy away from it." (Al-Bokhari)

A new appointee was sitting beside Omar(R), who was appointed by Omar(R) as a treasurer for one of the Muslim states. One of Omar's (R) little sons walked in during that meeting. Omar (R) kissed and hugged his son, which was surprising for the new appointee, so he told Omar (R), "I have many children, but I have never kissed them." Omar (R) immediately, suspended his appointment and said, "How can a person be generous with other people who has no sympathy and love for his own blood?" (Al-Farooq)

SEX EDUCATION

Sex education is the most misunderstood concept amongst Muslims. Most Muslim parents don't like to talk about sex with their children. They wrongly assumed that talking about sex or sexual topics with children is a big sin. Old-fashioned people consider it very disrespectful if and when children ask sex related questions. By not talking to them about sex, parents wrongfully assume and pretend that their children know nothing about it. This is a wrong assumption and has nothing to do with Islam.

Allah (S) has educated us about sex very clearly and explicitly in the Qur'an. We have received very thorough knowledge about sex from the books of Hadith as well. We also know every intimate detail between Mohammed (s) and his wives. Because Allah (S) wanted to guide us about sex, He taught us about its permissibility and prohibitions.

For example, reading and understanding the Qur'an is obligatory for every Muslim. It is a part of the parents' duty to teach the Qur'an to children beginning at the age of six or seven year. An eight or nine-year-old Muslim child should be able to read and understand the Qur'an. There are many occasions in the Qur'an where Allah (S) has described sex-related commandments. Consider an eight-year-old child (who understands the Arabic language) reads Sura Al-Yousuf, in which an unsuccessful rape attempts on Yousuf (A) is described. Moreover, (s)he reads Sura Al-Noor, Sura Al-Nisa, and other Suras in which the permissions and prohibitions of spousal intimacy have been mentioned. The child's innocent mind will have many questions about this intimacy.

"Parenting in Islam" By Javed I Khan

At this point, the child's mind will wonder for answers. If the child is scared of parents or the parents are not communicative in this respect, the child will find someone else for the answers, which could lead the child to misinformation and unhealthy sources.

If Allah (S) wanted to hide the sexual contents of the Qur'an from children, He would have rated different chapters (Suras) of the Qur'an. For example rated. Rated "G" Suras would have been for small children and rated "R" Suras for adults over eighteen. Or there would have been two Qur'ans: One for adults and another for children. As we know that there is only one Qur'an and none of the Sura in the Qur'an is rated. That implies that there is no secrecy about sex education in Islam. If we want to guide our children without raising them to be ignorant, we should educate them about the values of sex from the Islamic point of view.

If parents don't talk about sex with their children, and pretend that children know nothing about sex, they are wrong. This may have worked centuries ago, but not today. Internet is the biggest among the number of sex information resources are available to children. This information has access to the privacy of our own home. Almost every household has a computer or mobile phone, and every computer or phone is hooked up to the Internet, and every child has access to the Internet right from the family room in our house. Numerous websites offer access to audio-visual porno material on the Internet. In addition to Internet, TV or magazines, friends and other resources are out there to provide wrongful information and contaminate the innocent mind of our children that may force them into sinful habits. No Muslim parent would wants that to happen to their children.

"Parenting in Islam" By Javed I Khan

Sex is an important issue and should be addressed by parents directly. It is better that mother talks with the girls and the father talks with the boys. Starting at the age of five or six years, all questions about intimacy should be explained to children according to their level of understanding. Questions like, What is sex? When is it permitted in Islam? What is sexual morality in Islam? What are the requirements for sexual activity in Islam? These, and many other questions, should be answered as soon as children ask them or the parent feel children have those questions in their mind. More explicit information should be added, as they grow older. Children should also be told why premarital sex is prohibited in Islam. All questions should be answered from the Islamic point of view, not from our personal point of view. It is also appropriate for parents to correlate their Islamic viewpoints with the existing sexual diseases like AIDS, etc. Children should also be told that the existence of the dirty diseases is the punishment of Allah (S) on the people who do not follow His guidance on intimacy. And one can totally eliminate the chances of getting these diseases by following Islamic guidelines of sexual relationships. There are some exceptions to rules, however.

By equipping them sex education, we will be able to contradict all other misleading sexual information that might cause the sexual contamination in children's innocent mind. There will thus be a better chance that children understand better and rightful way of sex. May Allah (S) preserve our children from sexual misconduct (Aameen).

Of course, parents should possess a solid Islamic knowledge when they provide any answers to their children about intimacy. Otherwise, they might misguide their children instead. If parents do not have Islamic knowledge regarding sex or sex-related issues, they should educate them first or also contact a reliable Muslim scholar. Below are a few of many references from the Qur'an and Hadith about intimacy.

And those who guard their chastity, except with their wives and the (Captives) whom their right hands possess, for (them) they are not to be blamed, 70(29-30)

Narrated Abdullah (R): I asked the Prophet (s), "O prophet of Allah (S)! Which sin is the greatest?" He said, "To ascribe partners to Allah (S)." I asked, " What next?" He said, "To kill your child fearing of poverty." I further asked, "What next?" He said, "To commit adultery." (Al-Bokhari)

INTIMIDATION

To make their children listen and obey, many parents have a tendency to scare children with certain things, such as monsters, spooks, dinosaurs, bugs, darkness, and so on. Actually, fear of worldly things makes children cowardly and insecure. Parents should, instead, develop the love of Allah (S) in the children's minds. The person one loves the most, cares and respects the most and do not want to intimidate for the fear of anger. Children should, rather, be told that Allah (S) does not like bad things because they and He gets angry with whomever practices them. Or they may be told that certain actions displease Allah (S) so should not be practiced. Using the conscience of Allah (S), parents can make their children behave. This approach will also be able to develop a sense of good and evil in the children's minds. Tell the children that Allah (S) rewards good deeds, such as speaking the truth, listening to parents, respecting elders, and so on. This approach will make them mentally strong and they would not become cowards.

JUSTICE

If you happen to be a witness of your children's unlawful deeds, you are obligated to speak the truth against them in a court of law. Do not support your children against the law of you country. The Qur'an has taught us the same thing.

"O you who believe! Be you strong in justice, witness for Allah, even though it be against yourselves or (your) parents or (your) kindred, whether (the case be of) a rich man or a poor man, for Allah can best protect both (than you are). So follow not passion lest you lapse (from truth) and if you lapse or fall away, then lo! Allah is ever Informed of all what you do." 4(135)

"Parenting in Islam" By Javed I Khan

PHYSICAL PUNISHMENT

Physical punishment like spanking or hitting children is a very controversial subject of modern child psychology. Every child psychologist has his/her own opinion on this subject. Some psychologists are in favor of light physical punishment, some are in favor of mere spanking, and others are strictly against it. Besides all these ideas, Islam has taught us a unique concept on this issue. Islam teaches us that we are only allowed to spank our children if they are ten years or older and do not regularly practice prayer five times daily. There is no evidence in Islamic history when children had been spanked for any other reason. Let us examine the beauty of this approach.

As I mentioned early part of this book, children imitate in what they see their parents do. If they see parents implementing Islam in daily life, they will automatically be led to practice Islam. Islamic practices mean staying away from lies, from stealing, from gangs and drugs, corruption etc. Islamic practices also mean being good, obedient, kind, truthful, and straightforward. No parent would spank a child with good qualities.

If parents do not practice religion, however, children are not obligated to follow the Islamic values because they do not have any role model to follow. This type of parents will have no justification for spanking children. For example, if we do not pray five times a day, we have no right to spank children if they do not do so.

Parents of the modern age have different values of spanking. They may not, normally, spank their children for the sake of Allah (S) but only for worldly things. This, of course, is not permitted in Islam. Modern parents mostly spank children either when they do not listen or when they interfere in parents' interest. For instance, some parents may spank their children when they are interrupted during their favorite TV show, or when parents want them to go to bed and children do not, or when they break something expensive, or when they do not do their homework and so on. In Islam, there is no justification for spanking children for these, or any other, worldly reasons. Period.

We, however, are human and have a tendency to spank our children for many worldly reasons eventhough we know we should not. It is always better to ask for an apology from our children for this behavior. Some parents may feel embarrassed to ask for an apology from their children, however. Remember: this is another way of teaching them a lesson of accepting your own mistakes and willing to work on them.

"Parenting in Islam" By Javed I Khan

IGNOBLE CHILDREN

Trust is one of the strongest bonds between the members of a family. Trust is like glue that binds the entire family together. More trust leads to greater love that ultimately leads to closer interactions among the family members. Parents must trust their children without any doubt. Factoid doubt weakens bonds of love between the two. Some children are not trustworthy, however. Parents must keep up their trust that endeavors children to become a better person. The following reference from Sura Al-Yousuf also supports the same concept:

"Said the father, "My (dear) little son! Do not share your vision with your (step) brothers, they may plot a plot against you: Lo! Satan is an open enemy of men!" Verily in Yousuf and his brothers are signs for seekers. They said, "Truly Yousuf and his brother are loved more by our father then we: But we are good boys! Really our father is obviously wondering (in his mind)!"
(One of them said) "Kill Yousuf and cast him out to some unknown land, so the favor of father may be given to you alone: For you to be righteous after that!" Said one of them: "Do not kill Yousuf, but if you must do something, throw him down to the bottom of the well: He will be picked up by some caravan of travelers." They said: "O our father! Why do not you trust us with Yousuf, we are indeed his well-wishers? Send him with us tomorrow to enjoy himself and play and we shall take very good care of him." Yaqoob said, "Really, it saddens me that you should take him away: I fear that a wolf should hurt him while you do not attend to him." They said, "If the wolf dared to hurt him while we are a (large) party, then, indeed, we should (first) have perished ourselves!" So they did take him away and they all agreed to throw him down to the bottom of the well. And We inspired him that surely you shall tell them of their deeds while they knew not." 12(5,7-15)

"Parenting in Islam" By Javed I Khan

CONFRONTING BEHAVIOR

Confrontation is a very tricky subject in child-psychology. It can be addressed in a direct or an indirect way. The direct confrontation might make children aggressive, therefore, child-psychologists do not recommend this technique. Indirect confronting technique has been recommended by child psychologists. I have mentioned here an indirect confrontation method from Islam for the readers' knowledge. The first and most important lesson is to never confront your disobedient or misbehaving children right at the spot. Secondly never confront them without any solid evidence against them. Research the facts of the incident before you discuss the topic with your child. Also talk with them in private and listen to their side of the story. Let them express their point of view so you have both sides of the story. Once you know they are at fault, you should still give them the chance to prove themselves. If you see improvement, applaud their efforts.

Never lose your temper at the time of confrontation. Be calm and cool when talking with them about problematic situations. Highlight their good points to make them feel secure and safe. Do not condemn them by calling them names or otherwise insult them. Use appropriate language and wait for an appropriate time to talk with them. Provide logical reasons and solid evidence to make them realize that what they had done was wrong or immoral. Also provide solutions to their problems and show your willingness to work with them towards a better behavior.

The same method was followed by Yaqoob (A) (in Sura Al-Yousuf). When sons came to Yaqoob (A) crying and told him that a wolf killed and ate Yousuf (A) while they were playing out in a field, Yaqoob (A) knew that his sons were lying. Yet he did not condemn them, confronted them, or accused them of their lie. He probably lacked any evidence against them and he was afraid of their retaliation. Guess what might have happened if he had confronted them at that time? He would have made them angrier and that anger might have led them back to the well -into which they had thrown Yousuf (A)- and would have actually killed Yousuf (A). Instead, Yaqoob (A) just said, "I shall be amongst the steadfast."

"So they did take him away and they all agreed to throw him down to the bottom of the well. And We inspired him that you shall tell them of their deed while they knew not. Then they came to their father in the early part of the night, crying. They said, "O our father! we went racing with one another and left Yousuf with our things; and the Wolf ate him. But you are not going to believe us even though we tell the truth." They stained his shirt with false blood. He said, "Nay but your minds have made up a tale (that may pass) with you. (For me) Patience is most fitting: against that which you have done to me. It is Allah (alone) whose help can be sought." 12(15-18)

"O you who believe! Truly, among your wives and your children are (some that are) enemies to yourselves: so beware of them! But if you forgive and overlook, and cover up (their faults), verily Allah is often-forgiving, most merciful." 64(14)

SECOND TRUST

Allah (S) forgives us over and over again. Likewise, If children have betrayed your trust, do not make it the last time you trust them. No trust implies no more chances for improvement. Give them more chances of improve. Your next trust, however, must not be blinded like the first one. This time make a written agreement with them and let them know the reason for the agreement. Now is the time to tell them about previous mistrust and ask for your assurance of the current trust. This action of yours will make them more responsive and understanding. In Sura Al-Yousuf, the conduct of Yaqoob (A) and reaction of his sons are the reasons for my above statement.

'Now when they returned to their father they said, "O our father! We are not going to get more measure of grain for our brother (without him being with us). So send our brother with us that we all may get our measure. And we will indeed take very good care of him." He said, "Shall I trust you with him with any result other than when I trusted you with his brother before? But Allah is the best to take care of him. And He is the most merciful of those who give mercy!" And when they opened their baggage, they found their stock-in-trade had been returned to them. They said, "O our father! What (more) can we desire? Our stock-in-trade has been returned back to us by the ruler: so we shall get (more) food for our family; We shall take care of our brother; And add (at some time) a full camel's load (of grain to our provision). This is but a small quantity." Yaqoob said, "Never will I send him with you until you swear a solemn oath to me, in God name that you will be sure to bring him back to me unless you are yourselves hammed in (and made powerless)." And when they had sworn their solemn oath, he said, "Over all that we say be Allah the Witness and Guardian."' 12(63-66)

PRAYERS

In addition to providing children with the best possible amenities in life, the best possible education and training, lots of love, affection and care, parent's still need to do the most important part of parenting: Praying for the children to Allah (S). Pray for their true guidance, pray for their obedience towards you, pray for them to become good human beings, pray for them to be good Muslims, pray for them to stay at the right path, and so on. Start your prayer before their birth and continue until your death. Raising children without prayer is like cooking a meal without fire or heat or without any salt and spices. If you relied merely on your parenting skills and your own disciplinary efforts, you might be disappointed in the end. Allah (S) has told us how to pray for our children's guidance.

Below are the prayers of Prophets (As) of Allah (S) who prayed for their children's guidance and well being.

"O my Lord! make me one who establishes regular prayer, and also (raise such) among my offspring, O our Lord! and accept my prayer. "O our Lord! cover me and my parents with Your forgiveness: and (all) believers, On the day that the reckoning will be established." 14(40-41)

"And those who pray, "Our Lord! Grant unto us wives and offspring who will be the comfort of our eyes, and give us (the grace) to lead the righteous." 25(74)

"Parenting in Islam" By Javed I Khan

IMPASSE ADULT CHILDREN

You put forth the best of your efforts into guiding children, you tried to teach them the difference between right and wrong, and you prayed for them as much as you could; yet some of your adult children have still gone astray. Because Allah (S) did not want to guide them, they are going to be among the losers. You are helpless in this situation. You are not answerable to Allah (S) about their immoral, and sinful conduct. According to the Qur'an, impasse adult children are not a part of your family anymore, although they are genetically yours so let them go astray. Allah (S) told the same to Noah (A).

"At length, behold! there came Our Command, and the fountains of the earth gushed forth! We said: "Embark therein, two of each kind, male and female, and your family except those against whom the word has already gone forth, and the believers," but only a few believed with him." 11(40)

'So the ark sailed with them on the waves (towering) like mountains, and Noah called out to his son, who had separated himself (from the rest): "O my son! embark with us, and be not with the unbelievers."' 11(42)

'And Noah called upon his Lord and said: "O my Lord! surely my son is of my family and Your promise is true, and you are the justiest of judges." We (Allah) said: "O Noah! he is not of your family: for his conduct is unrighteous, so ask not of Me that of which thou hast no knowledge. I give thee counsel, otherwise you become one of the ignorant."' 11(45-46)

TESTS

As we know, this life is a test of Allah (S) for mankind. Power, poverty, health, youth, possessions, desires, and everything else including our children, are a part of Allah's (S) test for mankind. Let us see this fact from the Qur'anic point of view.

"Your riches and your children may be but a trial: Whereas Allah, with Him is the highest reward." 64(15)

"And you know that your possessions and your children are but a trial: And that it is Allah with Whom lies your highest reward." 8(28)

The death of children during the parents' lifetime, which is a very heart-breaking experience, is also one of Allah's (S) tests for human-beings.

Narrated Uns Bin Malik (R): The Prophet (s) said, "Any Muslim, whose three children died before the age of puberty, will be granted paradise by Allah (S) because of their (parents' patience on the death of their children) and His mercy on to them." (Al-Bokhari)

The following types of parents are mentioned in the Qur'an who are being tested by Allah (S) because of their children. I am sure that none of my readers fall under any of the following categories. If some parents do, this chapter will provide them with ample information so they could correct themselves through the mirror of Islam. Allah (S) may test parents in one or more of the following ways.

To some parents, perhaps, Allah (S) may have tested them

with a lot of wealth and corrupts children. The parents provide money to their corrupt children who spend that money in gambling, womanizing, drinking, and other sinful ways. These types of parents are equally responsible for their children's misdeed. An equal part of the children's ill deed is being accumulated into the parents' account unless they withdraw the financial support. These parents shall be interrogated and charged on the day of judgment for their financial support to their sinful children, even if those parents worship Allah (S) during nights, fast during days, and help needy.

"Let not their wealth nor their children dazzle thee (O Mohammed): Allah's wish is to punish them with these things in this world, and that their soul may depart while they are unbelievers." 9(85)

To some parents, perhaps, Allah (S) may have given wealth and an obedient yet less intelligent child. The parents desired to educate the child in order to hold a prominent position in society. They bribe for their child's education, for a higher degree, and for a good job. They might satisfy their conscience by justifying to themselves that they did not hurt anybody's feeling yet the are wrong. They have committed many sins: First of all, they bought a degree for an incompetent person and have thus created an incompetent so-called expert from their wealth. This, of course, is a wrong and immoral action. Secondly, their child took a position from a competent and deserving candidate for the job. Thirdly, they bribed other people and according to one Hadith, *"The one who gives and the one who receives bribe are a part of the hellfire" (AL-Bokhari).* Above all, the parents have set a bad example for the child. The child is an eyewitness to the parents' wrongdoing that made him lose parental respect. The parents have indirectly taught the child that he or she can get away with doing wrong things through wealth. They have ruined the child's faith in Allah (S) and have put his or her faith in money. No matter how good, kind, and generous these parents are, they have created a bad example for their child and they must be prepared to see the angry face of Allah's (S).

"As in the case of those before you: They were mightier than you in power, and more flourishing in wealth and children. They had their enjoyment of their portion: and you have of yours, as did those before you; and you indulge in idle talk as they did. Their works are fruitless in this world and in the hereafter, and they are the losers." 9(69)

To some parents, perhaps, Allah (S) may not have given enough wealth but may have given them physically strong children. They may brag about the children and they may feel proud of them. They may use them as a bully. The parents increase their wealth by wrong means using their children's strength. These parents are not on the path of Allah (S). If these parents use the strength of their children to save mankind, to help the needy, to spread the truth, and to support the good, they and their children would have been the strength of Allah (S).

"Then did We grant you (Jews) victory over them: We gave you increase in resources and sons, and made you the more numerous in man-power." 17(6)

"Let not their wealth nor their children dazzle thee (O Mohammed): in reality, Allah's wish is to punish them with these things in their lives, and that their soul may perish in their (very) denial of Allah." 9(55)

To some parents, who may be poor and have limited resources, but they are over caring parents. They may want to make their children happy and prosperous but their limited resources do not allow them to fulfill these desires. They steal, take bribes and use other unlawful means to increase their income. To them, their intention is good yet their action is not. They are using unlawful resources to support their children. They are wrong according to the Islamic point of view, they are wrong from a legal point of view, and they are morally wrong. They are not only causing a great damage to themselves, they are also ruining their children's faith by teaching them unlawful ways of earning a living. They are paving their own, as well as their children's, way towards the hellfire.

In the following lines, I am going to discuss some of the important facts about any of the above type of parents. These parents who have been mentioned in the Qur'an. Allah (S) has - indirectly- asked us these questions in the Qur'an, "Would you like to work hard without receiving proper recompense? Would you like to be punished for a crime you have never committed?" The answer to these questions is certainly, "NOT." Yet you may do so if the wealth that you have earned by hard work falls into the wrong hands after your death. Whether you have earned it lawfully will take you to hellfire on the Day of Judgment if your beneficiaries did not spend it correctly. At the time of your death, your beneficiaries shall be less worried about your burial and more about the splitting your wealth. Your children, spouse, and other loved-ones shall enjoy your money at the cost of your deeds on the Day of Judgment. Above all -on that day- they shall hide from you so you might ask for a return favor. See the reference below:

"O mankind! do your duty to your Lord and fear (the coming of) a day when no father will hide from his son, nor a son from his father. Verily, the promise of

Allah is true: let not then this present life deceive you nor let the chief deceiver deceive you about Allah" 31(33)

In addition, your children and spouse shall complain to Allah (S) against you that if they had not inherited your wealth, they would have been among the righteous. And if they had not been born in your home, they would have been better people. Therefore, you should be punished for their wrongdoing as well. They shall also claim -in front of Allah (S) on the dooms day- that you have set them on a wrong course in the worldly life. Then, my friend, you shall have no way to escape. You shall have no place to hide, you shall have nobody to support, and you shall have nobody to feel sorry for. See the reference below:

"It is not your wealth, nor your sons, that will bring you nearer to Us in degree: but only those who believe and work righteousness--these are the ones for whom there is a multiplied reward for their deeds, while secure they (reside) in the dwellings on high." 34(37)

"Of no profit to you will be your relatives and your children on the day of Judgment: He will judge between you: For Allah sees well all that you do." 60(3)

"O you who believe! let not your riches or your children divert you from the remembrance of Allah. And those who do so, surely they are the losers." 63(9)

"O you who believe! Truly, among your wives and your children are (some that are) enemies to yourselves: so beware of them! But if you forgive and overlook, and cover up (their faults), verily Allah is often-Forgiving, Most Merciful." 64(14)

Any parent who falls under any of the above-mentioned categories should be prepared for the anger of Allah (S) on the day of judgment.

On the other hand, there are parents who believe that Allah (S) is the real provider, that He has bestowed on them their children, and that He will take care of their needs too. If the parents do not have a good source of income, they must pray to the real Provider and He will open thousands of lawful sources of income for them.

"That it is He Who gives wealth and satisfaction." *53(48)*

"Of no profit whatever to them, against Allah, will be their riches nor their sons: They will be companions of the fire, to dwell therein (for aye)!" *8(17)*

PASSING THE TESTS

Like all other worldly tests, Allah's (S) test also needs some material for guidance and preparation material. The Qur'an is textbook or text material of guidance. According to the Qur'an, support your children within the guidelines of Islam. Support your children as long as they are obedient and good. Teach them to be good human beings and to stay on the straight path. Provide them from your lawful sources of income and fulfill all their genuine needs within your means. Let them know about your limitations and make them understand that they have to live within the limits. Do not go extra miles in the wrong direction for them. Do not support your children when they become criminals and wrongdoers. If they are not very diligent students, disobedient, unkind, or are not very good Muslims, pray for them and Allah (S) will open many doors for their success in this life and in the life hereafter.

Mohammed (s) said, "Three types of deeds stay with a person after death," one of them being good progeny. (Al-Muslim)

On another occasion, Mohammed (s) said, "A person will die with many sins and he will wake up without sins on the day of judgment. He will ask Allah (S) with a great surprise about his sins, and Allah (S) will answer him, 'You left good children behind who prayed for you and that's how We have washed your sins.'" (Tirmazi)

GENUINE LOVE

Let us think for a minute who really deserves most of our love: our spouse, who may marry somebody else after our death. Our children, who may split our property after our death. Or Allah (S), Who has blessed us a loving family, Who has given us a loving spouse, Who has bestowed us with health and wealth and all other amenities of life in this world? Mohammed (s) said, *"Allah (S) loves us seventy times more than our mothers."* When Allah (S) loves us that much, does not He deserve to be loved in return more than anybody else?

Narrated Omar bin Khattab (R): Some women and children among prisoners of war were brought before the Prophet (s). A women among them was milking her breast (her milk was flowing out of her breast and was making marks on her clothes while she was walking) and whenever she found a child amongst the captives, she tried to breast-feed the child. The Prophet (s) saw her and said to us, "Do you think that this lady can throw her child in a fire?" We replied, "No, if she has power not to throw her child in fire, she will not." The Prophet (s) then said, "Allah (S) is seventy times more kind and loving to mankind than a mother to her child. " (Al-Bokhari)

My friends, the love of Allah (S) and Mohammed (s) is the real and long-lasting love. This love will pay us back in this world and in the world hereafter. I do not mean that we should not love our children, spouse, and family. I mean we should love our children and spouse for the sake of Allah (S). Let us guide our families and ourselves that we should love Allah (S) and Mohammed (s) and Allah (S) will develop a strong, true and everlasting love among us. The following references shall give you some insights of love.

Mohammed (s) once said, "When somebody loves Allah (S) and his Messenger (s), Allah (S) orders angels to love that person and then he develops the love of that person in the heart of other people." (Al-Bokhari)

One lady brought her new-born baby to the Prophet (s) when he was leaving for a battle, and said, "Take my little son to the battle with you, O messenger of Allah (s)." The Prophet (s) replied, "How can I use this baby during the time of battle?" "Use him as a shield for you (from the arrows coming to hurt you) in the war," replied the lady. The Prophet prayed for both mother and son and returned the baby to the mother. (Al-Bokhari)

You will not find any people who believe in Allah and the last day, loving those who oppose Allah and His Messenger, even though they were their fathers or their sons, or their brothers, or their kindred. For such He has written faith in their hearts, and strengthened them with a spirit from himself. And He will admit them to Gardens beneath which rivers flow, to dwell therein (forever), Allah will be well pleased with them, and they with Him. They are the Party of Allah. Truly it is the party of Allah that will achieve success. 58(22)

PART III

RIGHTS OF PARENTS

PLEASING PARENTS

Many children of the modern world do not want to know their parents after they gain independence. It is a part of our religious and moral responsibility to please and take care of our parents under all circumstances. Moreover, we are guided to go a step further and please them not only in this life but after their death by treating their friends nice, by saying good words about them, and by praying for their forgiveness. Let us see what the following Hadith tells us about this situation:

One man asked Mohammed (s), "How can I please my parents after their death?" Mohammed (s) replied, 'Please your parents' friend and do good deeds.' (Al-Muslim)

"Parenting in Islam" By Javed I Khan

CHARITY

Always begin your charity from your own home. Your children, spouse, and your parents have more rights to your wealth than anybody else. Anything you spend on your parents, children, and family is counted as your charity in the eyes of Allah (S). Let us see what Allah (S) and His Messenger (s) has said in this regard.

"It is prescribed for you, when one of you approaches death, if he leaves wealth, that he bequeath unto parents and near relative in kindness. (This is) a duty for all those who ward off (evil)". 2(180)

"They ask thee, (O Mohammed), what they shall spend. Say: That which you spend for good (must go) to parents and near kindred and orphans and the needy and the wayfarer. And what so ever good you do, lo! Allah is aware of it." 2(215)

Once a man asked Mohammed (s), " O Prophet of Allah (S), I am a wealthy man, I have wife, children and parents. My parents are needy. Do I have to support my parents?" Mohammed (s) answered, "You and all of your possessions belong to your parents, because you are the property of your parents." (Abu Daud)

RESPECT

Whether they are illiterate, poor, uncivilized, narrow-minded, disabled, or non-presentable in any other way, parents always deserve to be treated with respect and honor. If you do not respect them, nobody else will. Generally, if people see you act disrespectful toward your own parents, they will not respect you and your parents. The Qur'an has discussed this issue many times. Following are the references from the Qur'an and the Hadith in this respect.

"We have enjoined on man kindness to his parents: In pain did his mother bear him, and in pain did she give him birth. The carrying of the (child) to his weaning is (a period of) thirty months. At length, when he reaches The age of full strength and attains forty years, He says, "O my Lord! Grant me that I may be grateful for Your favor which You have bestowed upon me, and upon both my parents, and that I may work righteousness such as you may approve; and be gracious to me in my issue. Truly have I turned to You and truly do I submit (to You) in Islam." 46(15)

"Such are they from whom We shall accept the best of their deeds and pass by their ill deeds: (they shall Be) among the companions of the garden: a promise of truth, which was made to them (In this life). But (there is one) who says to his parents, "Fie on you! Do you hold out the promise to me that I shall be raised up, even though generations have passed before me (without rising again)?" And they two seek Allah's aid, (and rebuke The son):" Woe to you! have Faith! For the promise of Allah is true." 46(16-17)

"Thy Lord has decreed that you worship none but Him, and that you be kind to parents, whether one or both of them attain old age in your life, say not to them a word of contempt, nor repel them but address them in terms of honor. And, out of kindness, lower to them the wing of humility, and say: "my Lord! bestow on them

Thy mercy even as they cherished me in childhood." 17(23-24)

"And kind to his parents, and he {Yahya (A)} was not overbearing or rebellious."
19(14)

Narrated Ibn-e-Amar (R): A man came to the Prophet (s) asking his permission to take part in Jihad. The Prophet (s) asked him, "Are your Parents alive?" He replied in affirmative. The Prophet (s) then said to him, "Then go and serve them."(Al-Bokhari)

    Nobody is perfect and neither are your parents. You may have certain grievances against them which could prevent you from being dutiful towards them. Don't let any grievance interfere in your service toward them.

    For example, if your parents were over caring, they were there to take care of you when you needed it. They were very understanding and generous towards you. They fulfilled all your genuine needs in your childhood. Yet you might be angry that they imposed very strict house-rules on you. They kept their eyes on each and every aspect of your life that made you think that they were very mean to you. You did not have any privacy and needed their permission for everything you wanted to do. They would let you do one thing but kept you from doing something else. Now you are a successful person but you still have some hard feeling about their behavior. Forgive their mean behavior because their tough attitude might have made you a successful person. If there were no hard and fast house rules, you might not have turned out so successful. I should like to share a short story that my father had told me when I was a little boy.

Once a King said to one of his wise ministers, "Show me the people who thought they had sweet parents and those who thought they had mean parents." The minister took the king to a market and pointed to a labor who was pushing a hand-cart and told the king that this person thought he had very sweet parents. Because his parents always fulfilled his demands. As a result, he did not learn to provide well for himself. He could not maintain the same lavish kind of lifestyle after parents' death. Now he was force to do a tough job for livelihood.

The minister pointed to another well-dressed person who was riding on a chauffeur-driven horse-cart and he was followed by many horse riders. The minister told the king that this person was now successful because his parents had very strict rules for him when he was growing up. He thought that he had very mean parents, but the rules he hated made him a successful person.

Likewise, your parents might have been very careless in during your upbringing. Perhaps they never guided you on how to lead a good life. They did not care whether you went to school or not. They did not pay attention to whether or not you kept good company or bad. You are a self-made person and you learned everything the hard way. Their carelessness might have made you into a more careful person. Their irresponsible nature might have transformed you into your current values. Their ignorance towards you might have made you aware of the toughness of the world. They, probably, did not know the way to guide or communicate with you. Perhaps they raised you the way they thought was best for you, or they did not know any better. Nevertheless, you should be caring toward your parents. You should respect their needs and feelings. You should still be kind, generous, and loving towards them. Never make them feel that they did not do any good for you.

"Parenting in Islam" By Javed I Khan

If your parents need you now and you are not there for them, then there is no difference between their action and yours. You are acting as they did. If so, every lesson you have learned to make yourself a successful person is worthless. Your self-achievement did not teach you how to be compassionate. You are as ignorant as your parents were. Let us compare our notes with the Qur'an and the Hadith.

"Say: come, I will recite unto you that which your Lord has made a sacred duty for you: that you ascribe nothing as partner unto Him and that you do good to parents and you slay not your children because of poverty. We provide for you and for them and that you draw not to lewd things whether open or secret. And that you slay not the life which Allah has made sacred, save in the course of justice. This He has commanded you, in order that you may learn wisdom."
6(151)

Narrated Al-Walid bin Aizar: I heard Abu Amr Ash-shaibani saying, "The owner of this house," he pointed to Abdullah's house, "said to me, 'I asked the Prophet (s), which deed is loved most by Allah (S)?'
He replied, 'To offer prayer at their early started time.'
Abdullah asked, 'What is next?'
The Prophet (s) said, 'To be good and dutiful to parents.' Abdullah asked, 'What is next?'
The Prophet (s) said, "To participate in Jihad for the cause of Allah (S).'
Abdullah added, 'The Prophet (s) narrated to me these three things, and if I had asked more, he (s) would have told me more.' (Al-Bokhari)

Above all, treat your parents the same way that you wish to be treated by your children in the future. If you think your children should look after you when you get old, look after your elderly parents. This is another way of teaching children to respect parents. If you don't have good relationships with your parents, do not expect your children to develop good relationships with you. Your children shall watch your each and every action towards their grandparents. So they may someday treat you the same way you have treated your parents. When I was a child, my father related a couple of stories to me which illustrate this situation:

A son decided to get rid of his elderly father by throwing him in a deep ditch. He took his father to the ditch and when was about to throw the father in, the father stopped him and requested the son to throw him in any other but this ditch. The son asked the reason. "Because I threw my father in this ditch when he was old and I was young," replied the old father. The son brought his father back and became very kind towards him and sought repentance from Allah (S).

On a cold night, a young father gave a very old, torn, and smelly blanket to his nine-year-old boy and told his to hand the blanket to his grandfather who was sleeping with cattle. The son returned after a while, his father asked if he had given the blanket to his grandfather. The son replied, "I have given half of the blanket to grandpa." "What did you do with the other half?" asked the surprised father, "I kept the remaining half for you, dad."

Sometimes a wife plays a very important role in mistreating her parents-in-law. She should understand that her husband is someone's son, and she shall be a mother and a mother-in-law one day. Following is a true story of one of my very close relatives:

A wife never let her husband support his parents. Whenever the husband wanted to send some money to his mother, the wife always resisted and told the husband, "Your children come first." Now she is old and has two sons. Both of the sons are very wealthy. Now she needs their support and whenever she asks her sons for support, the elder son reminds her of her own statement, "My own children come first, Mom. You have never let our father support his parents, why do you expect us to support you?" The following references from the Qur'an and the Hadith teach us the similar lesson.

"And serve Allah. Ascribe nothing as partner unto Him. (show) kindness unto parents, and unto near kindred, and orphans, and the needy, and unto the neighbor who is of kin (unto you) and the neighbor who is not of kin, and the fellow-traveller and the wayfarer and (the slaves) whom your right hands possess. Lo! Allah does not love the proud and boastful." 4(36)

"And when We made a covenant with the children of Israel, (saying): worship none save Allah (only), and be good to parents and to kindred and to the orphans and to the needy, and speak kindly to the mankind." 2(83)

Narrated Abu Bakra (R): The Messenger of Allah (S) said thrice, "Shall I not inform you about the biggest of the great sins?" We (the listeners) said, "Yes, O Prophet of Allah (S)" He said, "Assigning partners to Allah (S), undutiful to parents." The Prophet (s) then sat up after he had been reclining, and added, "And I (s) warn you against giving a forged statement and a false witness." The Prophet (s) kept on saying that warning till we thought that he would not stop. (Al-Bokhari)

EMBARRASSMENT

Some of us feel embarrassed by our parents, especially when they act in a way that shows their lack of education or their cultural differences from our educated friends. Most of the time, we are reluctant to introduce our friends to our parents because, we think, our parents might shame us. The following true story from the history of Islam gives us the same lesson:

Imam Abu Hanifa (r) was one of the four greatest Muslim scholars, whose description, explanation, and interpretation of Islamic law (Fikh) is followed by half a billion Muslims in the present world. He was so well-known, such a respected, and renowned scholar of his time that people used to travel thousands of miles to listen to his lectures and learn Islamic Jurisprudence from him. He used to deliver his lectures in an open field to provide room for five to ten-thousand students at one time each day. Yet whenever his mother wanted to get an answer to the question regarding Islamic Fikh, she would take the Imam to street-scholars with limited knowledge of Islam for their opinion on the subject. The Imam never hesitated or felt embarrassed by going to the street-scholars with his mother. He never said to his mother, "Ask me questions, if I can answer thousands of question every day for different people from all over the world, why can't I answer your questions? Or, at least, you should not bother to take me along to the so-called scholars."

Many street-scholars used to feel badly when they saw the great Imam of the time at their doorsteps with his mother desiring

"Parenting in Islam" By Javed I Khan

to ask a very simple Fika related question. They would tell the Imam that he was more knowledgeable in this matter than they were. But Imam always would say nicely, "My mother feels more comfortable with your decision, which makes me happier than anything else in this world."

ASSAILING PARENTS

Islam teaches us not only should we respect our parents, but pay respect to other people's parents as well. For example, if I do not like my spouse's parents for some reason and I talk badly about them. Generally speaking, I must not expect my spouse to respect my parents whether she likes them or not. In short, if you want people to respect your parents, you should respect yours as well as other people's parents. The following Hadith is a true reflection of my above statement:

Narrated Abdullah bin Amr (R): The Prophet (s) said, "It is one of the greatest sins that a man should curse his parents." The audience asked, " O Messenger of Allah (s)! How could a man curse his own parents?" The Prophet said, "A man curses the father of another man (during arguments or fights with one another), and the latter curses the father of the former (in return) and also curses his mother." (Al-Bokhari)

JUSTICE

Allah (S) has commanded us to be dutiful towards our parents within the legal limits only. We should not provide them any unlawful favor or try to hide the fact in the court of law even against our own parents. Hiding facts is not only socially and morally wrong, it is spiritually wrong as well. The liar will be punished on the Day of Judgment when we shall not find any helper. That day parents shall hide from children, spouses shall hide from each other, and children shall hide from parents. So, nobody should be asked for help. The Qur'an has mentioned this fact very clearly:

"O you who believe! Be you staunch in justice, witness for Allah, even though it be against yourselves or (your) parents or (your) kindred, whether (the case be of) a rich man or a poor man, for Allah is never onto both (than ye are). So follow not passion lest you lapse (from truth) and if you lapse or fall away, then lo! Allah is ever informed of what you do." 4(135)

KINDNESS TO MOTHER

Mohammed (s) said to his companions, "Paradise is underneath your mother's feet (Al-Bokhari.)" A Mother's love is the most merciful, the most blissful, and the kindest gift of Allah (S) for a person on the earth. This unique love cannot be defined or understood by anybody other than a mother herself. According to a famous saying, "When Allah created love. He kept ninety-nine percent for him and give one percent to his people. Out of that one percent from people, he gave ninety-nine percent to mothers and rest to every other soul. We have many duties towards our mother. Allah (S) has commanded us to be good to our mother three times more than to our father. No matter how much we have gain the fame of this world, be kind, polite, generous, and understanding towards our mother. There is an interesting story indicating the depth of a mother's love.

A man falls-in-love with a girl and proposes to her. The girl agreed on a condition that she would marry him only if he killed his mother and provided her the heart of his mother. He went and killed his mother, took out her heart and headed back to the girl. He tripped on his way back and fell down. The mother's heart spoke out, "Are you all right, my dear son?"

"He {Jesus(A)} said: "I am indeed a servant of Allah: He hath given me revelation and made me a prophet. "And He hath made me blessed wheresoever I be, and hath enjoined on me prayer and zakat as long as I live. "(He hath made me) kind to my mother, and not overbearing or unblessed. "So peace is on me the day I was born, the day that I die, and the day that I shall be raised up to life (again)." Such (was) Jesus the son of Mary: (it is) a statement of truth, about

"Parenting in Islam" By Javed I Khan

which they (vainly) dispute." 19(30-34)

"And We have enjoined on man (To be good) to his parents: In travail upon travail did his mother bear him. And in years twain was his weaning: (hear the command), "Sow gratitude to Me and to thy parents: To Me is (thy final) goal." 31(14)

Narrated Abu Huraira (R): A man came to the Prophet (s) and said, "O Prophet of Allah (S)! Who is more entitled to be treated with the best companionship by me?"
The Prophet (s) said, "Your mother."
The man said, "Who is next?"
The Prophet (s) said, "Your mother."
The man said, "Who is next?"
The Prophet (s) said, "Your mother."
The man said, "Who is next?"
The Prophet (s) said, "Your father." (Al-Bokhari)

Narrated Moghira (R): The Prophet (s) said, "Allah (S) has forbidden you to be undutiful to your mother, to withhold (what you should give) or demand (What you do not deserve), and to bury your daughters alive. And Allah (S) has disliked that you talk too much about others, ask too many questions or waste your property." (Al-Bokhari)

Narrated Usma bint Abu Bakar (R): My mother, who was still a non-believer and was divorced from my father, came to Medina (from Mecca) to seek my financial help. I went to seek the advice of the Prophet (s) {before I met my mother}. The Prophet said, "Yes, be good to your mother." (Al-Bokhari)

NURSING HOMES

Sending elderly parents to nursing homes is common in Western Society. Unlike sending children out for baby sitting, there is no precedence in Islam for sending old parents to nursing facilities. On the other hand, there are many occasions in the life of Mohammed (s) when he rejected people's request to participate in Jihad (Holy War) so they could stay home and serve their elderly parents. I have incorporated at couple of stories from the history of Islam in the last part of this book that indicate the importance of serving parents.

PRAYING FOR PARENTS

"When a person dies, nothing goes with the deceased except three things," said Mohammed (s). One of the three things is the deed of his/her righteous children,". Whether our parents are alive or dead, good or bad or whether we can get along with them or not, it is one of our important duties to pray for them. Always pray for them because your prayer adds into their good deed before and after their death. There is another Hadith where:

Mohammed (s) said, "A person dies as a greater sinner and he/she will wake up as innocent as a new-born baby at the Day of Judgment. The person will ask Allah (S), 'O Allah (S), I was a very sinful person at the time of my death. Why don't I feel the weight of my sins on my shoulders anymore?' Allah (S) will answer him/her, 'Because your children were good and they prayed for you so I have forgiven all of your sins.'"

We should not wait for parents' death before we start praying for their redemption from Allah's (S). The following commandments confirm my above statements:

"And Abraham prayed for his father's forgiveness only because of a promise he had made to him {Azar, the Abraham's father}. But when it became clear to him (Abraham) that he (Abraham's father) was an enemy to Allah, he (Abraham) dissociated himself from his father: For Abraham was most tender-hearted, forbearing." 9(114)

"O my Lord! make me one who establishes regular prayer, and also (raise such) among my offspring, O our Lord! and accept my prayer." 14(40)

"O our Lord! cover (us) with Your forgiveness, me, my parents, and (all) believers, on the day that the reckoning will be established." 14(41)

"Parenting in Islam" By Javed I Khan

"O my Lord! forgive me, my parents, all who enter my house in faith, and (all) believing men and believing women. And to the wrong-doers grant You no increase but in perdition!" 71(28)

"Forgive my father, for that he is among those astray." 26(86)

Narrated by Abu Huraira (R): A man came to the Prophet (s) and said, " O Prophet of Allah (S)! Who is more entitled to be treated with the best companionship by me?"
The Prophet (s) said, "Your mother."
The man said, "Who is next?"
The Prophet (s) said, "Your mother."
The man said, "Who is next?"
The Prophet (s) said, "Your mother."
The man said, "Who is next?"
The Prophet (s) said, "Your father." (Al-Bokhari)

PART IV

CHILDREN OF EARLY ISLAM

THE BEST FATHER

Sad Haaritha went back home after he bade farewell to his wife and his only child, Zaid (R). So Zaid (R) and the mother began an unfortunate journey with a caravan to visit her family. The caravan was raided and robbed during the course of its journey. Zaid's mother and a few other tribesmen had barely escaped. Zaid (R) and the others were captured by robbers and taken as slaves. The escapees told the whole story to Haaritha, who could not bear the fact that his only child was separated from them. He started a broad search for Zaid (R).

Zaid (R) was sold as a slave to a Meccan merchant. The merchant presented Zaid (R) to Khadijah bint Khawailud (R) and she gave him to her husband, Mohammed (s) (long before he became a Prophet), as a wedding gift. That's how young Zaid (R) got the opportunity to grow up in a noble family.

Many years later, on an occasion of HAJJ, Zaid (R) met a pilgrim from his hometown. The pilgrim gave him the news of the greiving parents and family. Zaid (R) sent a message of his whereabouts to his parents and family through the pilgrim. As soon as Haaritha received the message from his long lost son, he rushed towards Mecca with one of his brothers to free his son from the curse of slavery at any cost.

In Mecca, father and uncle greeted Zaid (R) warmly with tears, grieves, and sorrow, of many years' separation. They also met his master, Mohammed (s). They told Mohammed (s) the reason for their arrival in Mecca and offered to pay any price for Zaid (S) freedome. Although Mohammed (s) loved Zaid (R) very much, he respected the rights of the real parents. He told them,

"Zaid (R) has a freedom of choice. If Zaid (R) chooses to go with you, he may go without any ransom. I have no objection to that." They called Zaid (R) and gave him the choice. Guess what Zaid's (R) decided? He chose Mohammed (s) over his real parents and said, "My dear father and uncle, I am living with a wonderful person. He loves me more than any father would love his own son. He treats me like a prince. You would not have taken any better care of me than my master did. He always fed me before himself and he always took care of my comfort before his own. I cannot imagine leaving him." Although Zaid's father and uncle were surprised and disappointed, they were very touched that Zaid (R) was in wonderful hands. Mohammed's (s) eyes filled with tears. He immediately took Zaid (R) to the meeting-place -where all heads of the Meccan tribes discussed important matters- and declared Zaid (R) his son-by-adoption.

Zaid has a distinguished honor amongst all companions of Mohammed (s) that his name has been mentioned in the Qur'an.

"Parenting in Islam" By Javed I Khan

THE BEST MOTHER

Abdul Qadir (r), a four-year-old child, was brought to an Islamic school in Jilan, a city of Iraq. That was the first day of his regular school life. The child was very calm and quiet. His teacher brought him close, kissed his forehead and started to give him the first lesson from the Qur'an. The teacher recited the first verse from Sura Al-Fatiha -the first chapter of the Qur'an- and told the child to repeat it after him. But Abdul Qadir (r) had already learned the first full chapter by heart. The teacher was surprised and he started reciting "Al Bakarah" -the second chapter of the Qur'an. To the teacher's greater surprise, the child already knew that chapter by heart as well. The teacher asked the child, "Where did you learn all this when you have never attended any school before." Abdul Qadir (r) replied, "My mother has a habit of reciting the Qur'an out loud at home during her housework. I have listened to her from the day I was conceived and everyday thereafter. I memorized most parts of the Qur'an just by listening to her loud recitation every day." The child's response made the teacher cry. He said to the child, "Abdul Qadir (r), if all Muslim mothers bring up their children like your mother did, there is no way that followers of Mohammed (s) can go astray."

"Parenting in Islam" By Javed I Khan

THE FATHER OF NATION

A mad elephant was roaring in the downtown of Delhi, the Capital city of present India. A full army squad of the emperor was chasing after to capture the mad elephant but they seemed not to get any hands on the it. The people of the city were running like crazy on the streets to save themselves from the elephant. Like the day of judgment, nobody was worried about anybody or anything except the safety of his/her own life. A woman was also running with the flood of the people to save herself and her one-year-old boy whom she was carrying. Suddenly the boy fell off from her hands but she could not stop herself against the mad storm of the running people who were being chased by the mad elephant.

The little boy was crying in the middle of the street. Whose mother was shouting for help from the side-walk of the street. The people were running away from the boy and from the elephant, and the elephant was running towards the boy to crush the innocent soul under its gigantic feet. Nobody seemed to have the courage to save the little life from the mad monster.

Then people saw a man, who was hiding his face with a black turban, jump into the situation. Now the masked-man was between the elephant and the boy and the elephant was a few meters from the man. The man picked up the boy with his left hand and attacked the elephant with the sword in his right hand. His first attack on the elephant was so powerful and effective that the elephant changed its direction. Simultaneously, the army squad approached and trapped the elephant with chains. The hero's turban flew away due to the forceful attack on elephant and people were astonished to see that the hero was nobody else but their own Emperor, Zahir-Ud-Din Mohammed Babur, the Muslim Emperor of Sub-Continent of India,

"Parenting in Islam" By Javed I Khan

and the founder of the Great Muslim Mogal Empire in the Sub-continent. People were impressed and started thanking and praising him. He handed the child to the tearful mother and said, "The Emperor is like a father of his nation. I did not do anything special. I saved the life of my own child like every father would. "

THE WILL

When Omar Bin Abdul-Aziz (r), the fifth Caliph of Islam, died, Islamic history tells us that each of his children inherited just nineteen silver coins from their father's wealth because that was all he possessed. He was a Muslim ruler whose jurisdiction spanned over hundreds of thousands of square miles. Moslema-bin Abdul Malik (the Caliph's most trusted advisor) stated that at the time of his death, I said to the Caliph, "O leader of the faithful believers, I feel that you have always kept your children's mouth dry and you are departing this world with nothing for them. I wish you make me some will so I could give them some of my wealth." The Caliph replied, 'What you felt and said is wrong. I gave them their rights. I, however, did not give them anything beyond their rights. I shall not make any will to anybody about my children. I am leaving their matter with Allah (S). If my children are good and they fear Allah (S), Allah (S) will create sources for their income. If they turned out bad -on the other hand- I should not make them worst by leaving wealth for their bad deeds.'

The Caliph then sent for his children and said to them, 'O my children, I had two choices: either to make you wealthy through wrong sources and let you go astray, which is the way to hellfire for both of us. Or give you a good training so you can save yourselves from hellfire. Because I love you very much and I wanted to save you from hellfire, I did not accumulate any unlawful wealth for you. With the help of Allah (S), however, I have provided you the best possible training. I am confident that Allah (S) will provide you with everything if you prove to be among His faithful servants.'

"Parenting in Islam" By Javed I Khan

When Hisham-bin-Malik, the cousin of Omar-bin Abdul-Aziz (r), died, each of his children inherited more than ten million gold coins from father. Both of them, Hisham bin Malik and Omar-bin Abdul-Aziz (r), were the rulers of the same Islamic jurisdiction and died just three years apart. History is the witness of the fact that the children who had inherited nineteen silver coins from their father became so wealthy later in their lives that they used to donate hundreds of horses and camels for holy wars. And the children, who inherited millions of gold-coins from their father, ended up receiving charity from people. (Biography of Omar Bin Abdul Aziz)

O You Who believe! Take not for protectors your fathers and your brothers if they love infidelity about faith: If any of you do so, they do wrong. Say (O Mohammed): if it be that your fathers, your sons, your brothers, your mates, or your kindred, the wealth that you gained, the commerce in which you fear a decline, or the dwellings in which you delight are dearer to you than Allah or His Messenger and striving in His cause; then wait until Allah brings about His decision: And Allah guides not the rebellious. 9(23-24)

THE HAJJ

Abu Huraira, one of the prominent companions of Mohammed (s), would say goodbye to pilgrims (persons going to perform the pilgrimage of Hajj) with anguish. His friends used to ask him, " We know you can afford and you want to go for Hajj. What is stopping you from Hajj?" He would reply, "I have an old mother to take care of ." Friends would offer him money so he could hire somebody to take care of his mother while he would go for Hajj. He would always refused and did not perform NAFAL Hajj during the life of his mother.

Another Muslim Scholar -Kahsham Bin Hassan- received an offer from a friend to a hire someone to take care of his mother so he could go to Hajj. He rejected the offer and said, "My mother was there for me when I needed her as a child. Now she needs me and I will not go for Hajj leaving her under someone else's care."

"Parenting in Islam" By Javed I Khan

THE PATERNAL PRAYER

The father of the patient was the King of the most civilized country on the earth at the time. All health experts of the country including doctors, physicians, surgeons, homeopathicians, and alopathecians were in the palace to treat the patient. Religious authorities from various religions like Saints, Gurus, Sonth, Yogis, Priests, and Sanyases from all over the country were also in the palace. The Magicians, palmists, and astrologists were standing by with the patient as well. The patient was not a common man. The young crown prince Hemayoun, a son of the Muslim Ruler of the Subcontinent of India, was sick. The sickness of the prince was not simple either. Actually his case was very serious and hopeless. Each and every expert told Baber, the ruler of Indi, that they were not optimistic about the crown prince's life. They told Baber that, he too, should accept the fact that the crown-prince was about to die at any time. But Baber refused to accept the fact that his beloved son was going to die in front of his old eyes.

The King gave a final look to all health experts and ordered them to leave the palace. He then turned toward all magicians and let them go too. Finally he moved toward the religious authorities and said, "Do you have anything else to say besides that my son has no hope of life?" They all said, "Now is the time to pray for your son, your Majesty." This phrase is usually used for hopeless cases. It means no hope at all. The king said, "If prayer is the last answer for my child's life, I do not need anyone among you because I can pray to God like you do," and he let them go as well.

Now the King was alone in the room where Hemayoun was breathing his last. He looked at the dying face of his son and started walking around Hemayoun's bed. At the same time he prayed, "O Allah (S)! everybody in the whole kingdom is hopeless about the life of Hemayoun. I am not denying the fact of the death yet I refuse to accept the hopelessness from Your mercy. O Allah (S)! You are the Most Merciful and the Most Kind. O Allah (S)! I know that life span is fixed for everybody in this world and the life of my son seems almost over. O Allah (S)! Please give my remaining life to my son and I am ready to die in his place."

His prayer was answered immediately. When he finished seventh round around Hemayoun's bed, he felt weak and tired and sat on a corner of Hemayoun's bed. He could not get up from the same bed on his own and he died three days later. Hemayoun, on the other hand, miraculously recovered from his deadly disease and lived almost twenty years after the death of his father.

THE INNOCENT CONSPIRACY

The Prophet (s) used to organize the Muslim army outside Medina before they began their actual journey to the battlefield. While setting out for the battle of Ohad, the Prophet (s) carried out his usual organization just outside Medina.

Khudaij (R) asked the Prophet (s) if his son, Rafe (R), could be permitted to participate in the battle as he was a very good archer. Rafe (R) stood on his toes to make himself look taller than his actual height. The Prophet (s) allowed him to join the army. When Samarah (R) -Rafe's friend- learned about this, he complained to his father, Murrah (R), that the Prophet (s) had permitted Rafe (R) but not him to join the army, eventhough he was stronger than Rafe (R).

The Prophet (s) was informed of Samarah's (R) comments, who allowed Samarah (R) to prove his claim by fighting a friendly duel with Rafe (R). This was the duel of love, the desire to participate in Jehad, the wish to be killed in the path of Allah (S), and the love to obey the commandments of Allah (S). Samrah (R) murmured in Rafe's (R) ear while fighting, "Listen Rafe (R), you have already been granted permission by the Prophet (s) to participate in the battle. If you let me defeat you, I shall also be permitted to fight against the enemies of Allah (S)." As a result of this conspiracy, he defeated Rafe (R) and was permitted to stay with the army.

AN EAGER YOUNG SLAVE

Omair-bin-Saeed (R) was fifteen years old at the time of the battle of Khaiber. He was a slave of Abillahm (R). To fight in the battle of Khaiber, he went to seek the permission from the Prophet (s) to fight in this battle. Abillahm (R) recommended him very strongly to Mohammed (s) so he could participate in the battle. The Prophet (s) permitted him to participate in the battle and gave him a sword. Omair (R) was so young that he had to hang the sword around his neck and dragged it while he walked. Since he was a minor and a slave, he was not entitled to a full share in the booty. He knew that he was not going to get any share from the spoils of war, but he was still eager to fight in the battle. The Prophet (s), however, allotted him a special share from the booty. The motive behind this participation was to please Allah (S) and His Prophet (s).

"Parenting in Islam" By Javed I Khan

THE FIRST GRANDSON

Ommol-Fazal (R) -one of the Prophet's (s) Aunts- dreamed that a body part of the Prophet (s) was in her house. She got worried and the next morning went to seek interpretation of the dream from the Prophet (s). The Prophet (s) smiled after listening to her dream and told her, "Fatima (R), my daughter, will have a child and you will nurse him." Fatima (R) had her first child on the fifteenth of Ramazan, an important month in the Islamic calendar. As soon as the Prophet (s) heard this news, he rushed to his beloved daughter's home. The Prophet (s) kissed both mother and the newborn, then recited Azan (call for prayer) into the right ear and Iqaama (a call to start the prayer) into the left ear of the baby. Then he named the new born "Hassan" (R) (meaning beautiful). Hassan (R) was seven years old at the time of the Prophet's (s) death. In spite of his young, he is a narrator of quite a few sayings (Hadith) of the Prophet (s). Hassan (R) resembled Mohammed (s) so much that prominent companions of Mohammed (s) used to say, "We have not seen anybody walking on the earth who resembles Mohammed (s) more than Hassan (R)."

"Parenting in Islam" By Javed I Khan

THE FIRST BOY OF MEDINA

The Jews of Medina said that they had cast a spell on the emigrants preventing them from having a male child. The Muslims were very happy about his birth. Abdullah-bin-Zubair (R) was the first son born in a Muslim emigrant family one year after their migration from Mecca to Medina.

The Prophet (s) would not generally allow children to take an oath of allegiance to him. Zubair (R) had the honor of pledging allegiance to the Prophet (s) when he was only seven. During the battle against the Romans, he was barely in his twenties. He, alone, killed the commander of the Roman army who was surrounded by 200,000 soldiers.

THE BED OF DEATH

The night was very dark and full of horror and the house of the Prophet (s) was surrounded by the enemies of Allah (S). Their intention was to kill the Prophet (s) and to win the reward of five-thousand camels from Abu-Jahl, who Abu-Jahl had announced the reward of five thousand camels for killer of Mohammed (s). Gabriel, an angel from Allah (S), brought him Allah's (S) permission to migrate from the holy city of Mecca to Madian that night when the Prophet (s) was sleeping on his bed. This was the city of his forefathers, the city of his birth, and the city of Abraham (A) and Ismail. He told Ali (R) -his nineteen-year-old cousin- to sleep in his bed. Ali (R) knew that the house was surrounded by enemies who wanted to kill the owner of this bed. Ali (R) knew that this bed could be his last bed. Ali (R) knew that this night could be the last night of his life. Yet he slept in the bed of death without hesitation and let the Prophet (s) escape to Medina.

Later, someone asked Ali (R) whether he was ever afraid to sleep in the bed of the Prophet (s) that night, and if he knew he would be alive the next morning. Ali (R) replied, "I had no fear of sleeping on that bed, I instead had a deep and sound sleep of my life that night. When the Prophet (s) left for Medina, he told me that he would see me in Medina and I know that Prophet (s) always speaks the truth and Allah (S) will somehow save me from any harm." Ali (R) has the honor of being the first child who embraced Islam at the age of nine. He also has the honor to wed Fatima, the Prophet's (s) youngest daughter.

"Parenting in Islam" By Javed I Khan

GENUINE FEAR

Omar (R), the second Caliph of Islam, used to go out and look for needy people every night in disguise. One night he was on his usual night walk when he heard some noise coming out of a house. He approached the house and listened to the conversation coming from inside the house. He heard an elderly lady telling her ten-year-old daughter, "Add some water to the milk after you milk the cow. Nobody, not even Omar (R), is watching you." "I shall not add any water in the milk because Allah (S) is watching us. I am afraid of Allah (S) not Omar (R)," responded the daughter. The girl's answer touched Omar (R) a lot. The next morning, he sent a proposal for that girl to be his daughter-in-law. The proposal was accepted and the girl became his daughter-in-law. That girl became the grandmother of Omar Bin Abdul Aziz, the fifth Caliph of Islam.

"Parenting in Islam" By Javed I Khan

THE IRON MEMORY

Abu-Huraira (R) was another young companion of the Prophet (s) who is famous for his solid memory and his craving of learning Islam from the Prophet (s). He had the honor to spend four years of his youth with the Prophet (s). He was very devoted to the learning of Islam from the Prophet (s) and he did as much as he could to learn Islam during that period. He used to stay in the Prophet's (s) Mosque and used to listen to the questions put to the Prophet (s) by his fellow companions and used to memorize the Prophet's answers. His memory was so strong that once he was asked to describe a Hadith in front of a governor. The governor tested his memory with the same Hadith one year later, and Abu Huraira (R) described the same Hadith in exactly the same way he had done one year earlier. For this reason, a big portion of the Hadith has reached us from Abu Huraira's (R) iron memory.

THE YOUNGEST SAVIOR

It is very easy to follow the footmarks of someone in a desert. This was the biggest fear of Mohammed (s) and Abu Bakar (R), his companion, on the night of migration (the night Mohammed was ordered by Allah (S) to leave Mecca). Usma (R), Abu Bakar's ten-year-old daughter, took the responsibility of destroying the footprints of Mohammed (s) and her father by migrants with a herd of sheep until they found a cave to hide. She saved the life of Mohammed (s) and her father from Miccans. They stayed in hiding in the cave for seventy-two hours and the little girl kept grazing her sheep around the cave during that period.

The young savior brought food, milk and news from Mecca for the people in the cave. She also brought them camels so they could resume their escape after hiding. When she was packaging food for Mohammed (s) and Abu Bakar (R), she could not find any rope to tie up the food package. She then tore her scarf to tie the food. When Mohammed (s) saw her torn scarf, he smiled and called her Zatun-Nitaqain, which means the female with two scarves.

"Parenting in Islam" By Javed I Khan

THE YOUNGEST SOLDIER

Omair-bin-Abiwaqas (R) was a teenager who had embraced Islam in his early days. At the time of the battle of Badar- when the Muslim army was getting ready to depart from Medina- Omair (R) was trying to hide behind the older participants. He was afraid that the Prophet (s) might stop him from going to the battlefield because he was very young. Omair's (R) fear proved true. The Prophet (s) saw him and stopped him from going with the army. Omair (R) could not stand it and started crying. When the Prophet (s) heard him crying, he (s) permitted Omair (R) to participate in the battle. He was the youngest among the participants of the battle of Badar. Omair's (R) sword was too big for him. His brother, Saad Bin Abiwaqas (R), had to put a number of knots in the belt of the sword to make it fit young Omair (R).

"Parenting in Islam" By Javed I Khan

THE YOUNGEST IMAM

His hometown was on the way to Medina and Syria. All caravans traveling back and forth from Medina to Syria used to rest in his town. When Amar Bin Salma (R) was four years old, he heard a strange news from a caravan from Medina. The news was about a man, Mohammed (s) of Medina, who proclaimed himself a messenger of Allah (S). He would wait for the caravans coming from Medina so that he could ask questions about the Prophet (s). He asked questions such as, "What does he say, what does he do, what is his message and so on?"

He happened to meet some of the Prophet's (s) followers during that period. They related to him the basic teaching of the Prophet (s). They also said to him, "Mohammed (s) receives revelations from Allah (S)." One of them recited a few of the revealed verses in front of him. Amar (R) liked those verses very much. His innocent mind started learning those verses by-heart. From then on, whenever he happened to meet any of the followers of the Messenger (s), he would learn new verses and memorize them. It became a part of his regular routine later on. In this way, he memorized a good portion of the Qur'an, even before he embraced Islam.

At the time of the fall of Mecca, Amar (R) and his whole tribe embraced Islam. Many people of his tribe, including Amar (R), came to Medina to learn the teaching Islam from the Prophet (s). The Prophet (s) taught them the basics of Islam, these being prayer (Salaat), fasting and other obligatory commands. The Prophet (s) also told the tribesmen that the Salaat could only be led by an individual who possess the high degree of knowledge of the

Qur'an. This young boy was the person who knew the Qur'an more and better than anybody else in his tribe. Mohammed, therefore, appointed Amar (R), as an Imam by (s) eventhough he was only ten-year-old. He was the youngest Imam in the history of Islam in the life of the Prophet (s).

ANSWERS OF THE SELF-ASSESSMENT TEST

YES: 1, 4-8, 11, 13-15, 18-20, 23-35, 39, and 40.

NO: REST OF THE QUESTIONS

Self-EVALUATION

EXCEPTIONAL	100%
PERFECT	94%
GOOD	90%
NEED IMPROVEMENTS:	89% or LOWER

THE YOUNGEST RACER

One morning, Salma bin Akwah (R), a young boy, was passing by a small village called Ghabah, a few miles away from Medina, where the Prophet (s) used to send his camels to graze. The boy saw Abdur Rahman Fazari, a disbeliever, and his companions killed the keeper of the Prophet's (s) camels and drove the camels to their own village. The robbers were well-armed and were riding on their horses. Salma (R), on the other hand, was on-foot carrying his bow and arrows. He was such a good runner that he used to race with horses. He was also a very good archer. No sooner did he see the bandits, he climbed up on a hill and shouted towards Medina to inform people of the city about the crime. He then chased the bandits and started shooting arrows so quickly that the bandits thought they were being chased by a large group of people. If any of the bandits happened to turn his horse towards the boy, he hid behind a tree or any available shelter and inflicted wounds on the animal and bandits with his arrow.

The boy kept on chasing the bandits until all the camels - taken by the bandits- were left behind him. In addition, the robbers left thirty of their spears and thirty sheets of cloth behind them. Meanwhile, Oilniah-bin-Hisn, an another disbeliever, arrived at the scene to reinforce the bandits. After realizing that a single boy was chasing them, the bandits struck back at the boy from all directions. As they were about to reach the boy, he stopped them and engaged them in conversation until he received the help that he was expecting from Medina as a result of his early shout. Mohammed (s) was very happy with the bravery of the boy and prayed for his success.

"Parenting in Islam" By Javed I Khan

THE YOUNGEST INTERPRETER

When the Prophet (s) arrived in Medina, residents of the city brought their children to him (s) for blessing. Zaid (R), an eleven-year-old boy, was also brought to him for this purpose. The Prophet (s) was told that this boy was a multilingual. He could read and write Hebrew, Suryani and Arabic very fluently. From that day on, Zaid (R) became the secretary and the interpreter for the Prophet (s) in these languages. It was Zaid (R) who translated correspondences between the Prophet (s) and the Jews and many other tribes of Medina until the Prophet's (s) death. He has the honor to be the first and the youngest interpreter of the Prophet (s) and of Islam.

Zaid (R) was eleven at the time of Hijrah. He offered himself for the battle of Badar. The Prophet (s) did not permit him to participate in the battle because he was just thirteen. He volunteered for the battle of Ohad at the age of fourteen and once again his request was turned down by Mohammed (s). He became a regular soldier for Allah (S) after the battle of Ohad.

While the Muslim army was marching towards Tabuk, the flag of the Banu-Malik clan was held by Amarah (R). The Prophet (s) bade him to hand over the flag to Zaid (R), who was then eighteen-year-old. Amarah (R) thought that somehow he might have displeased the Prophet (s). So he asked the Prophet (s) the reason for the change. The Prophet (s) replied, "Zaid knows more Qur'an than you do. I give him preference over you because of his knowledge of the Qur'an."

"Parenting in Islam" By Javed I Khan

THE YOUNGEST NARRATOR

Hussain Bin Ali (R), Mohammed's (s) second grandson, was the son of Ali (R). He was one year younger than Hassan (R), his brother. He was a six-year-old boy at the time of the Prophet's death. Nothing much can be expected from a child of this age, yet we have received eight Hadith of the Prophet from this young boy. He is the youngest narrator of the Hadith.

Later in life, Hussain (R) refused to sign an Un-Islamic contract of the so-called Islamic ruler of that time. He and seventy-one members of his house holds including children and friends were assassinated at Karbala, Iraq for the treasons. He gave up his life but refused to bow down against the enemies of Allah (S).

THE CONQUEROR

An Arab ship was anchored at the port of Debal (now Karachi, Pakistan). The ship was carrying gifts for the Muslim Caliph which were sent by the Empire of Ceylon. The ship was also carrying Muslim men, women, and children pilgrims for Hajj. While at the port, Raja Dahir, the ruler of Sindh, looted the ship and took most of the passengers as prisoners. Some of the prisoners escaped and reported the incident to Hujjaj Bin Yousuf, the governor of Iraq. He immediately sent a message to the ruler of Sindh requesting the prisoners release. The Empire refused to take the responsibility of this loot and also refused to let the prisoners go. This was a great insult for the headstrong Hujjaj.

To rescue Muslims prisoners, Hujjaj sent out a Muslim army under the leadership of a courageous and steadfast seventeen-year-old, Mohammed Bin Kasim (r). Who had already proven his capable leadership under General Kutaiba (r) in central Asia. The young general not only conquered the land of Sindh and half of the Punjab up to Multan-Pakistan, he also captured the hearts of the people of that area. He treated people under his jurisdiction so well that the people of that area started crying and many Hindus made idols of him to worship as a god when he was called back by the Caliph. Islam reached into the sub-continent of India through the efforts of this young general Mohammed bin Kasim (r).

"Parenting in Islam" By Javed I Khan

THE YOUNGEST OFFER

In spite of knowing the strength of the Qureysh, Bara-bin-Azib (R), a twelve-year-old boy, sought the Prophet's (s) permission to participate in the battle of Badar. The Prophet (s), however, did not permit him to participate. He also offered his services to fight against the enemies of Allah (S) in the battle of Ohad, which took place one year after the battle of Badr. This time, too, he was too young to fight. After these two battles, he participated in every other battle against the disbelievers.

"Parenting in Islam" By Javed I Khan

THE YOUNGEST FOUNDER

When the Prophet (s) migrated to Medina, his three-year-old cousin, Abdullah (R), was already there to welcome him. From then on, the little cousin spent most of his time in the company of Mohammed (s) and tried to serve him by any means. One day, a few years later, Abdullah (R) brought the water of ablution for Mohammed (s). Mohammed (s) began to pray after performing ablution. The little Abdullah (R) stood behind him. Mohammed (s) made Abdullah (R) stand beside him (s), but Abdullah (R) went back to his previous place during the prayer. Mohammed (s) asked his little cousin after the prayer was over, "Why did not you stay beside me during prayer?" Abdullah (R) answered, "Because your personality is very great for me, I cannot imagine myself standing beside you, O Prophet of Allah (S)." His answer pleased Mohammed (s) and he prayed to Allah (S), "O Allah! give Abdullah wisdom." Mohammed's (s) prayer was answered.

Abdullah (R) become the founder of the school of tradition of Mohammed (s). After Mohammed's (s) death, he was the first person among the companion of Mohammed in the history of Islam who sought and kept records of the tradition of Mohammed (s). He started searching for Mohammed's (s) sayings from all possible sources. If he thought that a certain friend of Mohammed (s) knew some of Mohammed's (s) traditions, he would go to the house of that person and would wait outside without knocking at the door until the person would come out of his house on his own. He then would ask about the tradition of Mohammed (s). Many of them asked him, "O cousin of the Prophet (s)! Why did you wait outside that long for this simple question? You could have knocked at the

"Parenting in Islam" By Javed I Khan

door and asked." He would reply, "The thirsty person goes and seeks water, the water does not come to a thirsty individual." He became a member of Omar's Shoora Committee (the Muslim-Caliph's Advisory group of scholars) when he was sixteen. He was the youngest member of Shoora in the history of Islam. His pursuit of knowledge made him a well-respected authority on the Qur'an and on Islam. When Ibn-e-Omar (R) heard the news of Abdullah's (R) death, he said, "O-people of Medina! the death of Abdullah (R) is really the death of knowledge, not the death of an individual."

THE YOUNGEST GENERAL

It was not of any surprise for Mohammed's (s) companions when Mohammed (s) appointed Osama Bin Zaid (R), an eighteen-year-old boy, as the chief of the Muslim army which was going to fight against the army of Mosellema. Very close companions to Mohammed (s), such as Abu Bakar, Omar, and Sa'id Bin Abi Waqas (Rs), and others were also going with the army under this teenage general to fight the Mosellema's army. That courageous boy had proven himself in many earlier battles against the enemies of Allah (S). Each and every one of Mohammed's (s) companions liked the young boy so his appointment was greatly welcomed by them.

Worldly life of Mohammed (s) ended before the departure of the army. People suggested to Abu Bakar (R), Mohammed's (s) successor, that he should stop the departure of the army because of Mohammed's (s) death. Abu Bakar (R) rejected this suggestion. Other people suggested a change of leadership for the army. Abu-Bakar (R) again refused and said, "I can not dare to change the appointee of the Prophet of Allah (S)." The Caliph, however, asked the young general to spare Omar (R) to assist him, which the young general did.

The young general defeated the Mosellema's army, which was big, strong and well equipped in comparison with the Muslim army. This victory paved the ways for the conquest of Syria, Egypt and many other countries of the Middle East in the future.

THE YOUNGEST SCHOLAR

Aisha Siddika (R) was Mohammed's (s) youngest, and dearest wife, and spent ten years of her youth in the company of her husband. It was known that no one among the companions of Mohammed (s) had more knowledge of Islam than Aisha (R). She has narrated many Hadith. Especially, the Hadith about the domestic activities and the attitude of Mohammed (s) with his household came from Aisha. If it were not for her, Muslims would have lost one important aspect of Mohammed's (s) life.

She was so generous and giving that one day she received thousands of gold-coins from Omar (R), the second caliph of Islam. She gave away all that money in charity same day before the sunset. A maidservant reminded her that she had left nothing for herself and maidservant to break their fast. She said, "I wish you would have reminded me to save some for our breakfast before I gave away all money in charity."

"Parenting in Islam" By Javed I Khan

FORTY-GOLD-COINS

A caravan was robbed in the desert while heading to Baghdad, a city in Iraq. The possessions of the victims were taken away by the robbers. But the chief robber was not satisfied and wanted to make sure that none of the victims had any valuables left. So he started interrogating each individual of the caravan. Abdul-Qadir Jilani (r), a nine-year-old boy- who was traveling alone with the caravan. He was going to Baghdad for the sake of education because. Baghdad was the center for Islamic scholars at that time. - He was brought in front of the chief robber for interrogation. "Do you have any valuables in your possession?" The chief robber asked. The boy replied, "Yes, I have forty-gold-coins." "Where?" asked the chief. The boy pointed to the jacket he was wearing and said, "Here! My mother has sewn forty-gold-coins inside my jacket." The jacket was torn and forty-gold-coins were recovered. The chief was taken aback and told the boy, "You could have saved your money just by a simple lie." The boy's reply was very simple, "My mother taught me not to lie." The chief and other robbers were so moved by this answer that they began crying. The chief said, "Woe to me, I robbed and killed many innocent travelers. I disobeyed Allah (S) every moment of my life for the sake of money, and this little boy is ready to lose all of his possessions in order to obey his mother." The robbers returned everything they had looted from the caravan. They sought repentance from Allah (S) and became the boy's first disciples.

"Parenting in Islam" By Javed I Khan

TRUE FOOTSTEPS

When Abdullah (R) immigrated to Medina with his father, Omar bin Khattab (R), he was a ten-year-old boy and he was twenty at the time of the Prophet's (s) death. His contribution to Islam is unforgettable. He had the honor to spend about twelve years of his life under the direct supervision of the Prophet (s). He lived more than fifty years beyond the Prophet's (s) death and is one of the major transmitters of Hadith and Sunnah of the Prophet (s). If it were for not this young companion of the Prophet (s), Islam would have been deprived of many Hadiths and Sunnahs of Mohammed (s). Aisha (R), a wife of the Prophet (s), once said, "Nobody follows the footsteps of the Prophet (s) like Abdullah (R)."

One day, Ibn-e-Waa'il saw Abdullah (R) receiving four-thousand gold-coins (Durham) and a piece of velvet from Othman bin Uffan (R), the third Caliph of Islam. Next morning, Ibn-e-Waa'il also saw Abdullah (R) buying food for his family and his horse on credit. Out of curiosity, he went and inquired from the household of Abdullah (R) about the facts of money and credit. They told him that Abdullah (R) gave all the money away in charity on the day he had received it.

"Parenting in Islam" By Javed I Khan

MATERNAL IMPORTANCE

On his return from a Ghazwa (Battle in which Mohammed (s) has participated) one day, Mohammed (s) entered the vicinity of Medina. He took a deep breath and said, "His smell is still in Medina but he is gone." Mohammed (s) then added, "But he will be meet me in the world hereafter- not in this world." One of the companions asked Mohammed (s) that who the Prophet (s) was talking about. He replied, "I am referring to Ovais Karni (r). He loves Allah (S) and me very much. He is the best of all of my followers except my companions. Allah (S) will forgive hundreds of thousands of my followers just for the sake of Ovais Karni (r)." "If he is so much in love with you, why does he not come and stay in your company like we do, O-Prophet of Allah (S)?" asked a surprised companion. "Because he does not want to leave his old and blind mother alone. He does not have anybody else to take care of her. His mother let him go for some days so he could meet me. He came to Medina and missed me and left without seeing me just because he promised his mother that he would stay so many days in Madina," replied Mohammed (s). "Will anybody among us meet him?" asked another companion. Mohammed (s) replied, "None but Ali and Omar (Rs)."

Before his death, Mohammed (s) sent for Ali and Omar (Rs). He gave them his shirt and said, "When you meet Ovais Karni (r), give my shirt to him for me and request him to pray for the forgiveness of my followers." This historical fact indicates that taking care of elderly parents is more important than being in the company of Mohammed (s) in the eyes of Allah (S).

"Parenting in Islam" By Javed I Khan

TWO WEAK BOYS

In the battle of Badr, two young boys were standing one on either side of Abdur Rehman bin Auf (R), an eminent companion of the Prophet (s). He thought, "I would be safer in the battle-field if I were standing between strong and experienced worriers instead of two boys." Suddenly, one of the boys caught his attention and said, "Uncle, could you please show me who is Abu Jahl? I have heard that Abu Jahl is the worst enemy of the Prophet (s). I swear to Allah (S)' if I see him, I shall not leave until I kill him or I am killed." The other boy had a similar talk with Abdur Rehman (R) as well. Abdur Rehman thought that these boys were too young to kill Abu-Jahl, the head of the infidel army who was very well guarded. Abdur Rehman (R) promised to show them Abu Jahl, and he did, when he saw Abu Jahl dashing about on the battlefield on his horse.

Both of the boys immediately darted towards Abu Jahl and attacked him with their swords. The boys were on-foot, while Abu Jahl was riding on a horse. One of the two boys hit the leg of the horse and the other struck Abu Jahl. Both, the horse and Abu Jahl fell to the ground and the boys did not let him get up again. The boys were Maaz-bin-Amar (R) and Maaz-bin-Arfa (R).

"Parenting in Islam" By Javed I Khan

LOVE OF ALLAH (S)

Abu Saeed Khuzri (R) was thirteen when he requested his father to get him permission from the Prophet (s) to allow him to fight in the battle of Ohad. His father went to the Prophet (s) and said, "O Prophet of Allah (S), my son Saeed (R) has a very strong and well-developed body. He is also eager to fight against the enemies of Allah (S) in the battle of Ohad." The Prophet (s) disapproved his request and did not allow the boy to join the fight.

This young child approached the Prophet (s) through his father and that the father was not afraid of his son being killed in the battlefield. The father did not discourage his son from going to battle. He listened to his son and sought the Mohammed's (s) permission on a dangerous mission of death for his own son. That indicates that both son and father loved each other for the sake of Allah (S). They helped and encouraged each other just to please Allah (S) in their lives.

"Parenting in Islam" By Javed I Khan

BURN THE BOATS

"Burn the Boats," ordered the young chief of the Muslim army after each soldier had landed on the coast of Spain. Every Muslim soldier was surprised and wanted to know how this whole army would go back to their homeland. The young general read this question on the faces of soldiers so he added, "We either shall conquer Spain, or die. If we conquer the country, everything in the country, including their ships, shall be ours. If we die, we shall not need ships anyway." This talk encouraged the whole army and it was not long before the army conquered the whole country of Spain under the leadership of the young general. Tarik Bin Zeyad (r) is his name. He was in his early twenties at that time. The port Gibraltar, in Spain, is actually a modified form of JABAL-AL-TARIK (meaning Mount of Tarik) named after Tarik Bin Zeyad (r). It is mount where he had once said, "Bur the boats."

"Parenting in Islam" By Javed I Khan

Parenting In Islam

Printed in Poland
by Amazon Fulfillment
Poland Sp. z o.o., Wrocław

94514391R00092